Cooking with Friends

Cooking with Friends

EAT, DRINK, AND BE MERRY

CARLEY SHIMKUS

FOX NEWS books

CONTENTS

INTRODUCTION

One thing is certain. I have always absolutely loved food. And when you love something *this* much like I do, you can't be shy about it! That's why I'm so excited to share this book with you, my friends.

For those who tune in regularly to any cooking segment on FOX News, you'll know that I have no problem chowing down on camera. As a matter of fact, it's one of my favorite parts of the gig. I mean, where else do you have the opportunity to eat steak tacos or grilled ribeye at six thirty in the morning? Only on *FOX & Friends*!

As the story goes, my appreciation for food started at an early age. My parents, Ed and Zulma, have always described me as an "enthusiastic eater." Apparently, when I was little, I would push their friends out of the way at parties to get to the dinner table first. Hey, a girl's gotta eat, right? Fast forward to adulthood, and one of my fondest food memories takes place in Chicago. My husband, Pete, and I were dating at the time, and he had just gotten a job in the Windy City while I

First grade picnic. Mom always made the best sandwiches.

was still living in New York. One night, we decided to try deep-dish pizza, a Chicago staple. It was so delicious I genuinely cried some happy tears. The crust of the deep-dish pizza was similar to a flaky croissant, light, buttery, and so addictive. Then came about four inches of melted cheese (my guilty pleasure) and sauce. How could you NOT get emotional?

Now, pizza wasn't something I had a whole lot of as a kid. Both of my parents

*My first of many family seafood dinners.
I was about the same size as the lobster!*

are very much tied to their heritage, especially when it comes to food. And as I look back on my formative years, it's clear that my parents placed a BIG emphasis on home-cooked meals. Those meals and family time spent eating together are memories I cherish and something I'm excited about maintaining in my own growing family.

My mom's parents were born in Puerto Rico, and she grew up in a very traditional Puerto Rican household. I have fond memories of being upstairs in my room and all of a sudden getting the inviting whiff of her cooking. It was usually a Puerto Rican staple of rice and beans with a hearty stewed or roasted meat. My paternal side hails from Lithuania and Poland, and my dad happens to be an expert in the kitchen as well. Lots of kielbasa and pierogies were happily

consumed because of him, not to mention family favorites like cabbage rolls that also happen to be a staple for FOX's very own Dr. Marc Siegel.

When I was growing up in New Jersey, our family spent a lot of time at the shore, so fresh seafood was a staple. Honestly, there is nothing like a big bowl of linguine with clam sauce after a long day at the beach, and my dad's recipe for this classic is the absolute best. Trust me, you are going to want to turn to page 110 for this one.

So, you are probably noticing a theme—enjoying delicious food has served as a soundtrack to my entire life. As a matter of fact, food even played a supporting role in how I became interested in working at FOX News. When I was a teenager, *FOX & Friends* was always on while I was eating breakfast before school. I would become so interested in the show, I would sometimes forget to eat altogether. At night, family dinners were consistently spent in the company of FOX News programming as well. Yes, it's true, it was around the clock FOX at our house—something I have a feeling many of you can relate to. Because of those meals, and of course the message I was listening to on TV, I decided in high school I wanted with all my heart to work at FOX. Through a ton of work, persistence, and the blessing of God, my teenage breakfast dream became a reality. Truly, I thank Him every single day for the incredible opportunity.

So while I love eating and politics, the truth is my love for cooking was fostered more recently. To be specific, I would say that I got serious about cooking in 2020. Do you guys remember what happened in 2020? I digress from the politics, but as we all know, everything shut down because of the pandemic, and with some more time on my hands, I decided to expand my culinary horizons. There was just one problem, though. I was living in a very small New York City apartment that had a stove about the size of an Easy-Bake Oven with only one full-size burner. This led to some unique challenges, but I made due with what I had. For those readers who might be less accustomed to, or perhaps even a bit fearful of the kitchen, I have been in your shoes. But with some time and practice (and some help from Mom!), I learned to embrace and fall in love with the experience of cooking. And let me tell you, not all of my trials were successful—in fact, I might run out of pages describing some of my tribulations! But I'll give you a few.

My first Thanksgiving turkey was made in the Easy-Bake Oven (that's

My first-ever Thanksgiving Turkey

As Dad always says whenever there's seafood around, "when I 'see food,' I eat it."

Diving in at one of my favorite NYC restaurants— Jacob's Pickles.

her nickname) and it turned out pretty good! Lasagna, though, was a different story entirely. Did you know you shouldn't fill the lasagna pan ALL the way to the top? Apparently, when you

Seafood tower in New York City

Pizza in Chicago

Carrot cake in Boston

since I already made that mistake, you can enjoy some of the great lasagna recipes in this book without any fear that you'll have to call the fire department. Hot wings? Another fail. I'm still not even sure exactly what happened, but the wings wound up so insanely spicy Pete and I spent about an hour in tears before we decided to order takeout. Yet, even despite a few mishaps, I've discovered that cooking is all about persistence, and I'm enjoying my nightly journey of cooking and eating with a bit of Frank Sinatra in the background.

While I absolutely love talking all things politics on FOX *& Friends*, my favorite segments have always been "Cooking with Friends." When I was growing up, I loved watching the people I admired go from presenting serious news to letting their hair down on a lighthearted cooking segment. Now that I work on the show, I connect to the segments even more, not just because I get to eat, but because the people who are showcasing their favorite family recipes are now my real friends. And I genuinely love watching my friends share the food that makes them smile.

I know you love "Cooking with Friends" too. Many of you have told me. Recently, a woman named Carole sent me a hamburger-shaped hat and booties for my baby with a note saying how much

do, as it cooks it WILL bubble over and smoke will billow out of your oven into your apartment, setting off your smoke alarm and scaring your neighbors! Hey, you live and you learn, and fortunately, she loves the food segments. She also made mention of how enthusiastically I eat on TV. I got such a kick out of that gift—thank you, Carole! It's people like Carole and the stories that follow that make me so delighted to present this cookbook. While some days will always call for serious news, now you will have a reliable, go-to resource to reference, filled with wonderful recipes, history, and lighthearted stories from your favorite folks on FOX News—all in one place. How great is that!

Finding my own culinary approach, as well as sharing this cookbook, comes at a serendipitous time. My life so far has exclusively centered around my career and my wonderful husband, but this next phase is a big one. Pete and I recently welcomed our first child, a baby boy, into the world. Now, our little boy is our *entire* world.

Because of him, I couldn't be more excited to make family memories with the delicious meals I enjoyed while I was growing up, as well as share delightful recipes from my friends and colleagues at FOX News. What a gift that all of these exceptional people get to be a part of my kitchen and yours!

So, I invite you to dig in, literally, to the recipes and stories collected here as you work your way through this

The perfect day with my guy!

My sweet boy Brock. I love you as much as you love that bottle.

cookbook. I want this book to be well-worn, stained with food and drink, and scribbled with your own notes as you have just as much fun cooking through this book as I did putting it together.

And while there are few things I enjoy more than eating, I must admit, there is one thing that stands out above the rest:

Cooking (and eating) with friends. Cheers!

Chapter 1

BREAKFAST

FAMILY BREAKFAST

DAD'S MINI-PANCAKE TACOS AND MAMA'S CREPES

★ *Family-Friendly* ★ *Cheap Eats* ★ *Sweet Treats*

ABBY HORNACEK

HOST, FOX NATION

In our house, cooking up and sharing a big breakfast is a celebrated family ritual. But for me personally, there are two dishes, Dad's mini-pancake tacos and Mama's crepes that stand out the most. While my dad, Jeff Hornacek (a legendary NBA coach and player), knows his way around the basketball court, he's the first to jokingly admit that he's not "the best cook in the family." Dad describes his pancake recipe as a "weekend staple" in our house, "the easiest thing he knows how to make—something all the dads can make out there for the kiddos when Mom's away." While the recipe might be easy, I can attest it's also delicious. Making use of frozen pancakes is a great hack to turn out a sweet treat in no time. That said I will stress, however, that the proper eating technique is to roll up your sleeves, and eat these mini pancakes like tacos prior to devouring them. My mom, Stacy, on the other hand, always put in a little extra TLC to make her signature crepes for our family on Sundays. Using a blender to whip up the crepe batter (with a touch of vanilla extract—shhh, it's Mom's secret) ensures they come out smooth and consistent—but you could also go old school with a mixing bowl and a whisk. These two simple standouts provide a great game plan for a hearty, family-friendly start to the day.

DAD'S MINI-PANCAKE TACOS

Serves 4

12 frozen mini pancakes

1 cup semisweet chocolate chips

½ cup confectioners' sugar

1 tablespoon assorted sprinkles

1. Arrange the frozen pancakes into a single layer on a microwave-safe plate or platter. If necessary, the pancakes can be prepared in batches. Evenly top each pancake with approximately 6 chocolate chips. Place the pancakes into a microwave and cook on high for 45 to 60 seconds, or until the chocolate chips have nearly melted. Using a butter knife, spread the chocolate evenly on the top of each pancake.

2. To finish, sprinkle the pancakes with confectioners' sugar and assorted sprinkles. Fold the pancakes like tacos to serve.

MAMA'S CREPES

Serves 4 to 6

2 cups whole milk

4 large eggs

3 tablespoons unsalted butter, melted, plus more for greasing the pan

1 tablespoon sugar

1 teaspoon vanilla extract

½ teaspoon kosher salt

1½ cups all-purpose flour, sifted

1. Combine all of the ingredients in a blender and process until the mixture is smooth, about 20 seconds.

2. Over medium heat, lightly brush an 8-inch nonstick pan with additional butter. Add about ¼ cup of the crepe batter to the center of the pan. Lift the pan from the heat and, using a rolling motion, swirl the batter around the pan to thinly and evenly coat it all the way to the edges. Return the pan to the heat and cook the crepe for approximately 30 seconds.

3. Carefully flip the crepe and cook on the other side for an additional 30 seconds. Remove the crepe from the pan to a serving plate. Repeat until there is no more batter.

SWEDISH PANCAKES

★ *Family-Friendly*

JASON CHAFFETZ
CONTRIBUTOR,
FOX NEWS CHANNEL

For me, marriage turned out to be a sweet deal. This Swedish pancake recipe, a family favorite, was passed down from my wife's grandmother, Grandma Johnson. Grandma Johnson, who originally hailed from Sweden, was born in 1899 and touched multiple generations through her love of cooking. Heck, she even served as a professional chef in the U.S. military for two decades. And while I eat, it's my wife, Julie Chaffetz, who does most of the cooking in our house. Ironically, these pancakes have a consistency more similar to that of crepes, than traditional American pancakes. The main difference is that Swedish pancakes are a bit lighter and fluffier than crepes due to the fact they use less flour and more eggs and butter in the batter. These delicious pancakes can be topped with an array of your favorite ingredients from butter and syrup to jam or fresh fruit and whipped cream. I always tell people not to lay these flat, instead roll them up with your favorite toppings inside and enjoy. Oh, and don't be afraid to let them serve double duty, for both breakfast and dessert.

6 large eggs

4 cups whole milk

2 cups all-purpose flour

2 tablespoons vegetable or canola oil

2 teaspoons kosher salt

Spreadable butter, maple syrup, fresh fruit, jam, or whipped cream (optional)

1. In a large bowl, whisk together the eggs, milk, flour, oil, and salt until combined. If desired, an electric mixer can be used to blend them together.

2. Lightly spray a medium nonstick pan with cooking spray and place over medium heat. Pour about ¼ cup of the batter into the center of the pan. Lift the pan from the heat and, using a rolling motion, swirl the batter around the pan to thinly and evenly coat it all the way to the edges. Return the pan to the heat and cook for approximately 30 seconds.

3. Carefully flip the pancake and cook for an additional 30 seconds on the remaining side. Remove the pancake from the pan to a serving plate. Repeat until no more batter remains. Serve with toppings, as desired.

LEMON RICOTTA PANCAKES

WITH BLUEBERRIES AND WARM WISCONSIN SYRUP

RACHEL CAMPOS-DUFFY

CO-HOST OF
FOX & FRIENDS WEEKEND

&

SEAN DUFFY

CO-HOST OF THE BOTTOM LINE ON
FOX BUSINESS NETWORK

Sourcing local Wisconsin ingredients such as butter, cheese, and maple syrup is a key component of our family pancake recipe. It's a big family too, as Sean and I boast a brood of nine hungry children always ready to devour this breakfast staple. This pancake tradition began as a Saturday morning routine; it was super important to keep, especially when Sean returned home to Wisconsin from Washington, D.C. Of course, you don't have to be in our beloved Badger State to enjoy this tasty treat. I like to say that a meal is only as good as its ingredients, and working from that mantra, the key here is to use the best components possible, made better by supplementing the pancake batter with some surprises such as the ricotta cheese and lemon zest, which add a bit of heft and lightness at the same time. If blueberries are not in season, you can use thawed frozen blueberries if necessary. The trick is to use beaten egg whites to make these pancakes extra light and fluffy.

2 cups all-purpose flour

½ cup granulated sugar

2 teaspoons baking powder

½ teaspoon kosher salt

2 cups part-skim ricotta cheese

4 large eggs, whites and yolks separated

1 cup whole milk

2 teaspoons vanilla extract

4 teaspoons grated lemon zest

3 cups blueberries (see headnote)

TO SERVE

Confectioners' sugar

Unsalted butter, at room temperature

Maple syrup, warmed

1. In a medium bowl, combine the flour, sugar, baking powder, and salt, using a whisk to blend evenly. In a large mixing bowl, whisk together the ricotta cheese, egg yolks, milk, vanilla extract, and lemon zest. Slowly add the dry mixture to the wet mixture, whisking until evenly combined and smooth.

2. To finish the batter, beat the egg whites using an electric hand-held mixer until soft peaks form. Gently fold the egg whites into the pancake mixture until blended.

3. Grease a griddle or large cast-iron pan with cooking spray and place over medium heat. Pour about ¼ cup of batter onto the griddle for each pancake, working in batches if necessary. (Each pancake will spread to about 4 inches in diameter.) Scatter some blueberries on each pancake, reserving additional berries for serving, and cook for about 3 minutes, or until bubbles form on the outside of the cakes. Flip the pancakes and cook an additional 2 to 3 minutes, or until golden brown.

4. Remove to plates or a platter. Finish the pancakes with a dusting of confectioners' sugar and serve with butter, reserved blueberries, and warmed syrup, as desired.

AIR FRYER DONUTS & BUNNIES IN A BLANKET

★ *Family Friendly* ★ *Cheap Eats*

CHEF GEORGE DURAN

Boy oh boy, do I have some treats for you! Forget about spattering oil or waiting on your oven to preheat—for me, the air fryer serves a dual purpose in remaking a few of my favorite whimsical breakfast classics without the stress, or the mess. Since the air fryer gets hot with just the push of a button, you too can enjoy these dishes in no time without heating up the kitchen. These days, air fryers come in all shapes and sizes, as well as affordable price points to suit any budget. Their versatility makes them one of my favorite modern additions to my cooking equipment and repertoire. While I'm not personally a big fan of having tons of cooking gadgets, even I was surprised about how often I use my air fryer to reinvent some of my favorite foods, including these donuts and bunnies, bacon and other sides, and mains. And since we are skipping the oil and deep-frying altogether, perhaps this is one donut, or bunny, we can all feel good about enjoying in a second helping, or third!

AIR FRYER DONUTS

Serves 4 to 6

1 16.3-ounce can biscuit dough, such as Pillsbury

4 tablespoons (½ stick) unsalted butter, melted

1 cup sugar

2 teaspoons ground cinnamon

1. Remove the biscuits from the can and spread them out on a flat surface, such as a cutting board. Using an empty plastic water or drink bottle, invert the bottle to punch a hole in the center of each biscuit and shape the biscuits to resemble donuts. The dough removed to create the holes can be reserved to cook a separate batch of donut holes.

2. Add the donuts in a single layer into the air fryer basket. Depending on the size of your air fryer, you may need to cook in batches. Cook the donuts for 6 to 7 minutes at 350°F or until golden brown, turning halfway through.

3. Once the donuts have completed the cycle, remove them from the basket and allow them to cool for 60 seconds. Meanwhile, place the melted butter into a shallow bowl. Mix together the cinnamon and sugar in a separate bowl. Dip the donuts into the melted butter, followed by a dip in the cinnamon and sugar mixture. Serve immediately.

VARIATION: For a twist, you can dip your donuts into frosting and decorate with sprinkles instead.

BUNNIES IN A BLANKET

Serves 4 to 8

8 mini hotdogs

1 8-ounce can crescent roll dough, such as Pillsbury

1 large egg, beaten

Sesame seeds, for bunny eyes

1. Using kitchen shears, cut from one end of each hot dog two ¼ cuts from opposite corners to form "bunny ears." Remove the dough from the can and cut it into 1-inch strips. Wrap the strips tightly around each hot dog, leaving the "bunny ears" exposed, which will perk up when cooked. Brush the beaten egg on the dough and, working in batches as needed, add the dough-wrapped hot dogs to the air fryer.

2. Air-fry the hotdogs at 380°F for 8 to 10 minutes, or until the dough is golden brown. Remove the "bunnies in a blanket" to a platter. To finish, add two sesame seeds to the front to make eyes. Serve immediately.

ESSEX, VT
LIVE | 9:52 AM ET

FRENCH SCRAMBLED EGGS

★ *Cheap Eats*

CARLEY SHIMKUS

*W*hen you have time to savor your coffee and morning routine (a rarity with my hosting schedule), slow down your typical quick scramble for this version from our allies across the pond. We owe a lot to our French friends—from supporting the American Revolution, to the separation of powers, to the Statue of Liberty. Now, we can thank them for these eggs too! This method of scrambling and constantly stirring the eggs over low heat produces a porridge-like mixture of soft, fluffy eggs that go perfectly with a side of buttered and toasted baguette. Better yet, when cooked using this method, leftovers can be gently reheated without getting dry and tough. The key here is not to rush the process—the added effort and patience are worth the result. Also, use the best butter you can find—for the French (and those from the South), there's no such thing as too much butter! Not only does the butter help to create the right consistency, it also adds both fat and flavor to take these eggs to the next level, *oui, oui.*

Serves 4

6 tablespoons unsalted butter

12 large eggs, preferably at room temperature

1½ teaspoons flaky salt, such as fleur de sel

1 tablespoon finely minced fresh chives

1. Place a medium nonstick pan over low heat. Add the butter and allow it to melt slowly and become frothy, taking care not to let the butter brown. Meanwhile, whisk the eggs vigorously for at least 60 seconds to ensure they are completely beaten; there should be no visible egg whites in the mixture.

2. Pour the beaten eggs into the pan and stir constantly with a heatproof spatula for 10 to 15 minutes. After 8 to 10 minutes of stirring, the eggs will slowly congeal and begin to form small curds. If necessary, remove the pan from the heat in the final minutes to prevent the eggs from overcooking while stirring. The eggs are done once they have formed small curds, have thickened, and are still glossy and moist.

3. Transfer the eggs to a warmed serving platter or plate. Season them with the salt and garnish with the chives. Serve immediately.

GRILLED DONUTS

★ *Sweet Treats*

JANICE DEAN

**METEOROLOGIST,
FOX NEWS**

I like to live by a few mantras. First, life is too short, so have dessert first! Second, there are no rules! Such is the case with one of my favorite recipe twists. While I've rarely met a donut I didn't like, I realized that the only thing that can make a donut *better* is putting it on the grill. The trick here is that you have to buy glazed yeast donuts, not the cake ones, because those will fall apart on the grate. By slicing the donut to expose more surface area, adding butter (a lot!), and popping the donut on the grill, the sweet treat that we've come to love goes from just good to great in less than a minute. After that, the choice is yours—I like to create a toppings bar with an array of choices to finish these grilled donuts: from a cool treat like ice cream to caramel sauce to berries. One key piece of advice: Make sure you pay attention when that glazed portion of the donut hits the grill. Less is more here, as you only need a brief moment to pull off your new favorite breakfast—or dessert.

6 glazed donuts

6 tablespoons unsalted butter, at room temperature

1 pint vanilla ice cream

Fresh strawberries, raspberries, fudge sauce, caramel sauce, whipped cream, or other toppings, as desired

1. Preheat a grill over medium heat. Meanwhile, slice the donuts in half crosswise and spread each cut side with butter.

2. Next, place the donuts, cut side down on the grill for about 60 seconds. Flip the donuts to the glazed side and grill, uncovered, for 30 to 45 seconds, taking care that the sugar from the glaze does not burn. (Covering the grill and moving to indirect heat will prevent flare-ups.)

3. To serve, finish the warm donuts with a scoop of ice cream and your choice of toppings.

Carley's Corner: Out of all my co-hosts here at FOX News, Janice is definitely my go-to food buddy. We talk about food ALL THE TIME. In fact, our favorite mornings are when there is either free food, or we have enough time to order from the nearby diner. Janice loves a good BLT, while my go-to is a big breakfast burrito filled with eggs, onions and peppers, sausage, cheese, and salsa. Beyond our "breakfast buddy" friendship, Janice is one of the nicest people I know and makes me laugh constantly. I'm so blessed to have her as a friend.

SMASHED AVOCADO TOAST

★ *Healthy*

CARLEY SHIMKUS

It's no secret that avocados and toast are kin like peanut butter and jelly, but in recent years, this combo has become a cult classic. Creamy avocados provide the perfect texture when spread over crusty toast to help you make the most of any start to the day. I like to put my own spin on this dish, amping up the flavors of this modern breakfast (or any meal, for that matter) with an array of ingredients to suit a variety of tastes. Good avocado toast starts with ripe avocados—the peel of a ripe Hass avocado will be darker and give to the touch when light pressure is applied. Instead of simply slicing the avocados to top the toast, I like to smash the avocados with a fork or spoon to create a creamy, guacamole-like texture that provides a base to catch the rest of the toppings. The key here is also the toast—source a good country-style or sourdough loaf and slice your bread as wide as your toaster will accommodate to provide that thick crunch. I've laid out some of my favorite topping ideas, but feel free to pick and choose to make this toast your own.

Country-style or sourdough bread, cut into 4 thick slices

2 ripe Hass avocados

½ teaspoon kosher salt

½ teaspoon garlic powder

1 teaspoon fresh-squeezed lemon juice

1 large hard-boiled egg, peeled

½ teaspoon crushed red pepper flakes

¼ cup crumbled feta cheese

2 tablespoons good-quality extra virgin olive oil

Thinly sliced radish

Dill fronds

1. Toast the bread slices in a toaster until golden brown.

2. Use a paring knife to carefully cut lengthwise around the avocados, then open them and remove the pits. Using a spoon, dig out the avocado flesh into a bowl, discarding the skins and pits. Next, add the salt, garlic powder, and lemon juice and use the back of a fork to smash the seasonings into the avocado mixture until smooth, or to your desired consistency.

3. Generously spread the avocado mixture evenly on top of each piece of toasted bread. Next, use a fine grater to grate the hard-boiled egg evenly over the toast. To finish, top the toasts with the red pepper flakes, feta, and a drizzle of olive oil. If desired, garnish with sliced radish and dill fronds. Serve.

TATER TOT CASSEROLE

★ *Family-Friendly* ★ *Cheap Eats* ★ *Entertaining* ★ *Comfort Food*

CARLEY SHIMKUS

Craving a simple casserole? That's the name of the game with this hearty dish, which can be doubled and tripled as you like to stretch and serve the masses. Tater tot crowns, or rounds, cook up quickly to a crispy texture and serve as a crunchy base in this savory masterpiece. The key is to par-bake (partially bake) the crowns while you are finishing the prep. This extra step makes sure that the crowns have enough time to cook on their own, prior to being incorporated into the rest of the mix. If you want to spice things up, you can use a hot ground sausage or add a few dashes of your favorite hot sauce to the egg mixture prior to cooking. And don't skimp on the sour cream, folks—that extra bit of tang and texture provides a nice contrast to this savory egg bake. For more variation or personalization, you can use a blend of mozzarella, Colby, or Jack cheeses—including pepper Jack to kick it up a notch.

Serves 6 to 8

15 ounces or half a 30-ounce bag of frozen tater tot crowns or rounds

1 pound mild breakfast sausage, preferably Tennessee Pride

¼ cup finely diced onion

12 large eggs

1 teaspoon kosher salt

½ teaspoon fresh-cracked black pepper

2 cups grated sharp cheddar cheese

¼ cup sour cream

1 tablespoon finely sliced fresh chives

1. Preheat the oven to 425°F. Grease a 9 × 13-inch sheet pan and add the tater tots to the pan in a single layer, if possible. When the oven is hot, par-bake (partially bake) the tater tots for 6 minutes. Remove from the oven.

2. In the meantime, brown the sausage in a medium pan over medium heat, using a wooden spoon to break the meat up. After 5 minutes, add the onions and continue to cook until the sausage is completely browned and the onions are translucent, 4 to 6 minutes.

3. Distribute the sausage mixture evenly over the par-baked tater tots. In a medium bowl, whisk together the eggs and season with the salt and pepper. Pour the egg mixture over the sausage and tater tots. Top the egg mixture with the shredded cheese and, using a teaspoon, dollop the sour cream evenly over the dish.

4. Return the sheet pan to the oven and bake the casserole until the eggs are firmly set, 15 to 20 minutes. Allow to cool for 10 minutes. Garnish with the sliced chives and serve.

Chapter 2

LUNCH

CUBAN TACOS

★ *Entertaining* ★ *Comfort Food*

SARA CARTER
CONTRIBUTOR, FOX NEWS

While I love the thrill of traveling the world and chasing down lead stories, I must admit, there's not much I enjoy more than cooking this dish at home with my family. My mother came to America from Cuba in the 1960s on the Johnson Freedom Flight, so these tacos are not only tasty, they are also nostalgic and culturally important. Nowadays, even my daughter Analiese will stress that cooking these up is a delicious way to pay homage to her family heritage—a win for me in the mom camp! It's no secret that tacos are a favorite quick meal celebrated worldwide, and this variation, using a Cuban-inspired marinade and seasonings, provides another delectable variation on this beloved classic. While my recipe is a tried-and-true standard, you can change things up as you wish and make these tacos your own. For me and my husband, Marty Bailey, a wounded veteran who is also blind, cooking is a way for us to connect not only in our marriage, but by exposing our family to other cultures and cuisines. And as a busy mom, I am always looking for superhero tricks to save time and effort, so putting this dish together in a slow cooker lets me tackle my busy workdays knowing that I've got a delicious, family-friendly meal ready to serve at home.

Assemble the tacos by adding the chicken, beans, and plantains to the tortillas. Allow everyone to finish their tacos with the cheddar, sour cream, and cilantro as desired and enjoy.

Chicken, Cuban Style (recipe follows)

Black Beans (recipe follows)

Sweet Plantains (recipe follows)

24 small corn tortillas, warmed

TO SERVE

4 cups shredded white cheddar cheese

2 cups sour cream

1 cup chopped fresh cilantro

CHICKEN, CUBAN STYLE

4 large boneless, skinless chicken breasts

1½ cups freshly-squeezed orange juice

⅓ cup freshly-squeezed lime juice

2 teaspoons low-sodium soy sauce

2 teaspoons honey

3 tablespoons minced onion, sautéed in olive oil

2 teaspoons ground cumin

1 teaspoon dried oregano

1 teaspoon kosher salt

¼ teaspoon ground black pepper

1. Place the chicken breasts in a slow cooker. In a medium bowl, combine the orange and lime juices, the soy sauce, honey, onion, cumin, oregano, and salt and pepper and mix until combined. Pour the mixture over the chicken breasts.

2. Cover the slow cooker and cook the chicken on low for 4 to 6 hours. Turn off the heat and, using two forks, shred the chicken prior to serving.

BLACK BEANS

2 teaspoons olive oil

½ cup diced yellow onions

2 tablespoons diced green bell pepper

1 garlic clove, minced

1 14.5-ounce can black beans, drained and rinsed

½ teaspoon kosher salt

½ teaspoon ground cumin

½ teaspoon dried oregano

Place a medium pot over medium heat and add the oil. When the oil begins to shimmer in the pan, add the onion, bell pepper, and garlic and sauté for 4 to 6 minutes. Next, add the beans followed by the salt, cumin, and oregano. Stir to combine, adding a few tablespoons of water to help loosen the mixture. Reduce the heat to low and simmer the beans for 10 to 12 minutes. Remove from the heat and allow the beans to thicken and cool slightly prior to serving.

SWEET PLANTAINS

2 plantains (about 1 pound total), peeled and cut into ½-inch rounds

½ cup packed light brown sugar

¼ cup vegetable oil

1. Dredge the cut plantains on both sides in the brown sugar and set aside.

2. Place a large nonstick pan over medium heat and add the oil. Add the plantains in the oil and, using a fork, gently mash them slightly to help flatten them as they fry, about 2 minutes. Flip the plantains and fry them on the remaining side, about 2 minutes. Transfer the fried plantains to a wire rack lined with parchment paper to cool before eating them.

BAD DAY SOUP

★ *Family-Friendly* ★ *Comfort Food*

BRIAN BRENBERG
CONTRIBUTOR, FOX NEWS

When my wife, Krista, and I were having our first child, a friend of Krista's divulged this quick recipe to help get through some of the inevitable bad days ahead. I think any parent (or even a professor like me) can agree, some days are harder than others with kids, especially in those early years. Of course, this meal is meant to be a simple relief to get dinner quickly on the table. And even though these days our clan has grown to a family of five, this soup still remains a family favorite that I enjoy a few times a week. For me, the best part is that I was totally clueless about the "bad day" title until a few years after the tradition started—meaning that it was always a good day when I got served bad day soup at home! I suppose life is all about having perspective. For a variation, the ground beef can be substituted with ground turkey or chicken. If you like wild game, ground venison or bison can also work. Using V8 juice ensures a well-seasoned base that's loaded with all the good stuff that will make tomorrow a better day indeed.

2 tablespoons vegetable oil

3 medium onions, chopped

2 cups chopped carrots

1 pound ground beef

1 cup chopped fresh parsley, plus more for garnish

1 64-ounce bottle V8 juice

1 10.5-ounce can cream of chicken soup

1. Add the oil to a large stockpot over medium-high heat. Add the onions and carrots and sauté them for 8 to 10 minutes, or until just tender. Next, add the beef, crumble it with a wooden spoon, and cook until the meat is well browned, 6 to 8 minutes. Drain the excess liquid from the pot, stir in the parsley, and finish by adding the V8 juice and cream of chicken soup.

2. Bring the mixture to a boil, stir well, and reduce the heat to low. Allow the soup to simmer for 30 minutes before serving.

KALE POWER SALAD

★ *Healthy*

GERRI WILLIS
ANALYST,
FOX BUSINESS NETWORK

When I was first diagnosed with cancer, I decided to open up to our viewers about it; after all, we are all family here at FOX. I shared the tough news of my diagnosis and told everyone not to be sad—that I would be back. "Never give up" became my song, and searching for words upon my return to FOX, I simply uttered, "I'm back." That was a powerful moment, and this power salad, as I like to call it, became a comforting dish that I perfected as I battled and prevailed over my diagnosis. Eating well-balanced, nutritious food became a regular routine for me during that journey, something that I still stick to today. Loaded with colorful superfoods like sweet potatoes and kale, this hearty salad is both filling and satisfying. In the old days, kale was more of a garnish on a plate or buffet, but it's finally getting its due, showing up on restaurant menus all across the country. If you've never tried it, or didn't like it the first time you did, trust me, I'm going to make you love it! To get the best results, I like to add a bit of salt and olive oil to the chopped kale, then massage the greens by hand to help soften them prior to drizzling my tangy vinaigrette over the salad. The smoky garbanzo beans add a good bit of protein, along with a texture that's both creamy and crispy, from frying up in the skillet.

4 medium sweet potatoes, peeled and cut into 1½-inch cubes

½ cup extra virgin olive oil

2 teaspoons kosher salt

1 teaspoon fresh-cracked black pepper

2 15.5-ounce cans garbanzo beans, drained and rinsed

1 teaspoon curry powder

1 teaspoon chipotle paprika

¼ cup sun-dried tomatoes, packed in oil

8 cups roughly chopped curly kale, ribs removed and cut into bite-sized pieces

Vinaigrette (recipe follows)

¼ cup pumpkin seeds

1. Preheat the oven to 400°F. Arrange the sweet potato cubes into a single layer on a baking sheet, drizzle the potatoes with ¼ cup of the olive oil, and season with 1 teaspoon of the kosher salt and the fresh-cracked pepper. Using your hands, toss the sweet potatoes to ensure they are evenly coated by the oil. Bake the potatoes for 20 to 25 minutes. Allow to cool.

2. Meanwhile, add the remaining ¼ cup olive oil to a cast-iron skillet over medium-low heat. Add the garbanzo beans, curry powder, and paprika, mixing to combine, and cook for 15 minutes, stirring on occasion. Next, stir the sun-dried tomatoes into the sweet potato mixture and cook for 5 minutes. Remove the pan from the heat and allow to cool.

3. Place the kale into a large salad bowl and season with the remaining 1 teaspoon kosher salt. Using your hands, massage the kale in the salt for 30 to 45 seconds. Add the sweet potatoes to the kale, followed by the garbanzo bean and tomato mixture.

4. Drizzle the vinaigrette over the kale salad, tossing until well combined. Top with the pumpkin seeds and serve.

APPLE CIDER VINAIGRETTE

¼ cup extra virgin olive oil

2 tablespoons apple cider vinegar

1 small shallot, peeled and finely diced

1 tablespoon maple syrup

Whisk together all of the ingredients in a small bowl. Use immediately, or cover and store in the refrigerator up to 1 week.

GERRI'S RECIPE FOR HER COMFORTING KALE SALAD

FOX&friends

FOX NEWS channel

SUNDAY LUNCH CHICKEN SOUP

★ *Healthy* ★ *Family-Friendly* ★ *Comfort Food*

STEVE HILTON
CONTRIBUTOR, FOX NEWS

Forget about the politics, I really want a cooking show. Come turn the cameras on, as this is a dish that we make nearly every Sunday in the Hilton household. And while this recipe is basically chicken soup, it's unique because you cook a whole chicken and eat the whole chicken, so it's a full meal too. So, call it what you will, but this all-in-one comfort classic involves just a few simple steps to yield a delicious and wholesome broth. The key is to use a quality bird that weighs no more than 3 to 4 pounds, which will keep it nice and tender. My market often has larger birds, so I typically source a free-range or organic chicken, which is usually the right size for this meal, or a small fryer. Searing the chicken in garlic oil and splashing it with vermouth for some extra flavor requires just 10 minutes to prep, a nice time-saver for my schedule. After that, you load your favorite vegetables around the chicken—seriously, dealer's choice here on the veggies—followed by a few hours of roasting in the oven. You can serve this over cooked rice (my favorite), buttered noodles, or a cooked grain like quinoa or farro. Trust me, the comforting smell of this dish cooking in the oven is sure to make your Sunday afternoon even more special.

3 tablespoons garlic oil or extra virgin olive oil

1 3- to 4-pound chicken

3 tablespoons white vermouth, such as Noilly Prat

1 large onion, chopped

4 large carrots, chopped

4 parsnips, chopped

4 sticks celery, chopped

4 leeks, chopped and thoroughly rinsed

1 bunch Italian parsley

3 tablespoons kosher salt

3 tablespoons black peppercorns

1 bouquet garni of herbs such as rosemary, thyme, bay leaf, and parsley

Hot cooked rice, for serving

1. Preheat the oven to 400°F. Using your hands, press down on the breastbone of the chicken to help flatten the bird. Heat the oil in a large Dutch oven (an oval-shaped one works best) over medium heat. Next, add the chicken, breast side down, and let it brown for 5 minutes. Add the vermouth, flip the chicken and brown the other side for 5 minutes. Meanwhile, add the onion, carrots, parsnips, celery, leeks, parsley, salt, peppercorns, and the bouquet garni to the pot around the chicken as it is browning.

2. Next, add water to cover the chicken by at least 1 inch. Cover the Dutch oven and cook in the preheated oven for 2 to 2 ½ hours, until the chicken is fall-apart tender.

3. Remove the pot from the oven, and using tongs, remove the chicken to a cutting board and the vegetables to a dish. Allow the chicken to cool for at least 10 minutes, then using tongs or two forks, shred it into small chunks to serve alongside the vegetables, discarding any skin and bones. Strain the broth remaining in the pot and reserve.

4. To serve, place a portion of cooked rice in the bottom of each bowl. Next, add 4 to 6 ounces each of the chicken and vegetables. To finish, top with as much reserved broth as desired and serve.

Carley's Corner: Don't sleep on Steve's restaurant recommendations, as he is always a great person to ask when it comes to tracking down good food. Before a trip to London, he recommended that I try The Holly Bush in Hampstead, and it did not disappoint!

END-OF-SUMMER BLT SANDWICHES

CARLEY SHIMKUS

I often like to say that life, and food for that matter, is just a matter of which season you are in. And celebrating the season is one of the best ways to savor a variety of good food year-round. Take tomatoes, for example, which taste best when grown on the vine and picked at their peak. As the summer comes to a close, tomatoes really shine, getting even sweeter and meatier in their final days. When that day arrives, folks, make haste, put this classic and foolproof BLT sandwich together, and celebrate. We all know that bacon makes everything better—but believe it or not—there is one method of preparing bacon that reigns supreme. Baking bacon in the oven is foolproof; it turns out crispy every time. Plus, I like to reserve the bacon drippings (a Mason jar works best) to add a smoky kick to scrambled eggs, sautéed greens, or a batch of cast-iron cornbread.

8 strips thick-cut hardwood smoked bacon

8 slices country-style bread, toasted

4 tablespoons mayonnaise, preferably Duke's

2 vine-ripened heirloom tomatoes, thinly sliced

1 tablespoon everything bagel seasoning

4 leaves baby romaine lettuce

Potato chips, for serving

1. Preheat the oven to 400°F. Arrange the bacon slices on a parchment-lined baking sheet in a single layer. Bake the bacon, uncovered, until crispy, 15 to 18 minutes. Place the bacon on a paper towel–lined plate to drain excess grease.

2. Spread mayonnaise on each piece of toast. Next, arrange sliced tomatoes on four of the bread slices and season them with the bagel seasoning. Top the tomatoes with one piece of lettuce, two slices of bacon, and the remaining slice of bread. Serve the sandwiches with potato chips on the side.

HEGSETH FAMILY MINNESOTA WILD RICE SOUP

★ *Family-Friendly* ★ *Comfort Food*

PETE HEGSETH
CO-HOST, *FOX & FRIENDS WEEKEND*
&
PENNY HEGSETH
HIS MOTHER

This is home right here! A comforting soup on a winter day, especially in my chilly home state, Minnesota. This dish is a regular in our family. In fact, it's one of my mom Penny's signature recipes. While I'm not too much of a gourmet, a quality chicken stock, preferably homemade, will take this dish from good to great, so be sure to source (or make) the best you can find. My mom always adds ham to this soup for a smoky flavor, but you can use bacon or chicken instead. While you can source ham that's already been pre-cut or cubed, I always prefer to buy a ham steak that I cut myself—in my humble opinion, the texture comes out superior, not to mention it will yield leftovers you can fry up alongside some eggs for a post-workout meal later in the week. My mom, Penny, cooks this dish a couple of different ways, so I've provided her traditional method for making this soup on the stove here, and her crockpot version too! If you wish to make the latter, simply cook the ingredients in a crockpot for 3 hours, adding the half-and-half as the final step to gently heat it. I like serving this dish with some crusty buttered bread on the side.

Serves 6 to 8

½ cup wild rice

6 tablespoons unsalted butter

1 medium onion, chopped

2 garlic cloves, minced

⅓ cup all-purpose flour

4 cups chicken broth

½ cup diced carrots

3 tablespoons slivered almonds

¾ cup cubed ham (see headnote)

1 teaspoon fresh-cracked black pepper

1 teaspoon kosher salt

1 cup half-and-half or substitute heavy cream for a richer, thicker soup

Grated Parmesan cheese (optional)

1. Prepare the rice according to the package instructions. Let the cooked rice sit, covered, for 30 minutes.

2. In a Dutch oven, melt the butter over medium heat. Add the onions and sauté for 5 to 7 minutes, or until tender. Add the garlic, stir, and cook for 30 seconds. Next, sprinkle in the flour and, using a wooden spoon, stir it into the onion mixture to make a paste and let cook for 1 minute. Gradually pour in the chicken broth, stirring to incorporate the flour paste into the broth. Add the carrots, then increase the heat to medium-high and allow the mixture to come to a boil for 1 minute. Reduce the heat to low, stir in the almonds, ham, reserved rice, salt, and pepper and simmer for 5 minutes.

3. To finish, add the half-and-half and heat until warm.

4. Sprinkle Parmesan cheese over the soup, if desired, and serve.

Carley's Corner:
I've shared a lot about my penchant for eating on set—but we often joke that the only person who likes to eat on set more than me is Pete!

MEDITERRANEAN CHICKEN KABOBS

WITH HUMMUS AND TABOULI

★ *Healthy* ★ *Entertaining*

JEANINE PIRRO
CO-HOST, *THE FIVE*

This well-balanced Mediterranean-inspired meal is both hearty and healthy. While I was born and raised in New York, my parents actually hail from Beirut; my father was a mobile home salesman and my mother a department store model. Thus, this Lebanese-friendly dish pays homage to flavors from the homeland, and it's one that I cook up in regular rotation. The kabobs are delicious when quickly marinated, but if you have extra time, prep the kebab ingredients the day before so that they have extra time to soak up the flavor. For me, leveraging the food processor comes in handy to quickly whip up the tabouli and hummus as sides. If you've never made hummus at home, my recipe is a great intro to how simple it can be. As you gain experience, you can add additional quantities of your favorite items, to suit your tastes. In a pinch for time—we've all been there—feel free to substitute your favorite store-bought hummus instead of making your own. (Shhh, your secret is safe with me!) Tabouli is a Middle Eastern salad made from a base of parsley, bulgur wheat, and herbs. For me, it follows the same guidelines as a good spaghetti—both are great when enjoyed immediately, but taste even better as leftovers the next day.

MEDITERRANEAN CHICKEN KABOBS

Serves 6

1 pound chicken breasts, cut into 1-inch cubes

1 red onion, cut into 1-inch pieces

Green and red bell peppers, seeds and ribs removed, cut into 1-inch pieces

2 cups cherry tomatoes

¼ cup extra virgin olive oil

2 tablespoons red wine vinegar

1 tablespoon kosher salt

1½ teaspoons fresh-cracked black pepper

Twelve 8-inch wooden kabob skewers, soaked in water to prevent burning

1. At least 1 hour prior to grilling, add all the kabob ingredients, except the skewers, to a resealable plastic bag and place in the refrigerator to marinate for 1 hour, or overnight.

2. Prepare a direct charcoal fire over medium-high heat or preheat a gas grill for 10 minutes with the dials set to medium-high heat. Meanwhile, skewer the kabob ingredients evenly onto the skewers, being careful not to overcrowd.

3. Grill the chicken kabobs for 3 to 5 minutes on each side, for a total of 12 to 20 minutes, or until the chicken reaches an internal temperature of 160°F according to a meat thermometer. Remove from the grill and serve immediately.

HUMMUS

2 15.5-ounce cans chickpeas, drained and rinsed

Juice of 3 lemons

1 teaspoon kosher salt

2 garlic cloves, minced

1½ tablespoons tahini paste

Combine all ingredients in a food processor and pulse until smooth and creamy.

TABOULI

2 green onions, trimmed and cut into 4-inch pieces

2 sprigs fresh curly parsley, stems trimmed

¼ cup loosely packed fresh mint leaves

½ cup extra virgin olive oil

Juice of 3 lemons

1 teaspoon ground cinnamon

1 teaspoon kosher salt

½ teaspoon fresh-cracked black pepper

6 Roma tomatoes, ends trimmed and cut in half

1 cucumber, cut into chunks

1 pound ground bulgur wheat (#2 size), soaked in water and drained

Combine the scallions, parsley, mint, olive oil, lemon juice, salt, and pepper in a food processor and pulse until roughly chopped. Finish by adding the tomatoes, cucumber, and wheat to the food processor and pulsing a few times, until the cucumbers and tomatoes are chopped. Remove the tabouli to a serving bowl.

BLACK BEAN SURFER BURRITOS
WITH PICO DE GALLO

★ *Healthy* ★ *Entertaining*

GRIFF JENKINS
CORRESPONDENT, FOX NEWS

A once-a-week staple in our family, this is a dish that I picked up from my days spent surfing, from Costa Rica to California. Tough gig, I know! An array of burritos and tacos were always served when we came off the beach, making this burrito one of my favorite post-surf snacks with friends. Preparation is key. I like to prep the pico and other accoutrements prior to working the grill so that I don't lose focus. And using whole marinated chicken breasts ensures that they will get plenty of char from the grill without drying out. The homemade pico recipe can be adjusted to your taste; add a bit more jalapeño pepper if you want more spice, or more cilantro (a key ingredient for me) for that fresh herb flavor. The pico comes together very quickly, and it adds a nice cool and crunchy contrast to the savory chicken and beans. Once you've got all the components grilled and prepped, it's all about assembling and rolling up the burritos, with your favorite toppings on the side. You can even wrap these burritos in some foil just like we did back in the day on the beach. So, what do you think? Do you prefer Chipotle or Jenkins? The former has a nice ring to it, if I do say so myself!

1½ pounds boneless, skinless chicken breasts

½ cup extra virgin olive oil

Juice of 1 lemon

1 tablespoon kosher salt

1½ teaspoons fresh-cracked black pepper

1½ teaspoons garlic powder

Leaves from 1 sprig thyme

1 splash red wine vinegar

1 6- to 8-ounce package Mexican-style rice

1 15-ounce can low-sodium black beans

6 large flour tortillas, preferably La Banderita, warmed

TO SERVE

Pico de Gallo (recipe follows)

Shredded sharp cheddar cheese

Hot sauce, if desired

Sour cream

1. Place the chicken, olive oil, lemon juice, salt, pepper, garlic powder, thyme, and vinegar into a resealable plastic bag and marinate for 30 minutes, or up to overnight.

2. Prepare a direct charcoal fire over medium-high heat or preheat a gas grill for 10 minutes with the dials set to medium-high heat. Meanwhile, cook the rice in a medium pan according to the package instructions. In a small pan, warm the beans over low heat, stirring occasionally.

3. Remove the chicken breasts from the marinade, shaking off the excess. Grill the chicken over direct heat, 5 to 7 minutes per side, depending on the thickness of the breast. Flip the breasts and cook for an additional 5 to 7 minutes, or until the chicken reaches an internal temperature of 160°F on a meat thermometer. Remove it to a cutting board and let rest for 10 minutes. Cut the chicken into bite-size pieces or strips.

4. Assemble the burritos, placing the layers of rice, beans, and chicken on the lower third of each warmed tortilla. Top with the pico de gallo, shredded cheese, hot sauce, and sour cream as desired. Fold the ends (about 1½ inches) of the burrito over the toppings. Next, roll the burrito, working from the bottom side where the ingredients are provisioned, until tightly wrapped. Serve immediately.

PICO DE GALLO

1 heirloom tomato, finely diced

½ small white onion, finely diced

½ jalapeño pepper, finely diced

Juice of 2 limes

¼ cup chopped fresh cilantro

1 pinch of salt

Combine all the ingredients in a small bowl and stir until evenly incorporated.

GRIFF'S BLACK BEAN CHICKEN SURFER BURRITOS

Carley's Corner: Griff was the very first person I met at FOX News back when I got started in 2008. I was interning at the DC bureau, and I always thought it was so cool that Griff would take time out of his day to talk with me and the other interns. I quickly learned that Griff's thoughtfulness is one of his most contagious qualities. Perhaps my favorite memory is when we hosted the New Year's Eve (2019) show together. The whole experience was hilarious, including me "crowd surfing," thanks to the support and encouragement of Griff.

ARROZ CON POLLO

(CHICKEN AND YELLOW RICE)

★ *Cheap Eats* ★ *Family-Friendly* ★ *Comfort Food* ★ *Entertaining*

KURT KNUTSSON
GUEST, FOX NEWS

Growing up in the Tampa Bay area of Florida, I was always surrounded by Cuban culture and food. Though admittedly I'm sort of a mutt of Swedish heritage, this dish has become a family favorite, making me an honorary Cuban. Arroz, or rice, is one of the staples of Cuban cuisine; whether served with beans, chicken, sausage, or on its own, it's hard to find a Cuban plate without some arroz at its base. My mom, Maggie, is known for always putting her own special spin on this classic dish, such as adding some additional chicken into the mix so that I could gain that extra protein advantage in the gym. It's also a comfort meal that she cooks up to serve kids at the Ronald McDonald House in Tampa. That said, if you wish to cut down on the portions, you can pull off this recipe with just one chicken. Our family is pretty sporty, and this hearty dish is not only a big family and crowd pleaser, but it also transports quite well for a tailgate party or a potluck in the neighborhood. If you want to compete with the Knutssons (I dare ya!), you could cook this dish up in a big paella pan, as its large surface not only helps you tackle this whole dish in one pot, but it also lets your guests feast with their eyes prior to digging in.

Serves 8

½ cup extra virgin olive oil

2 small fryer chickens, about 3 pounds each, each cut into eight pieces

2 small onions, chopped

2 medium tomatoes, chopped

1 green bell pepper, seeds and ribs removed, chopped

4 garlic cloves, minced

4 cups chicken broth

2 cups long-grain white rice

½ teaspoon saffron threads

1 bay leaf

½ teaspoon kosher salt

¼ cup chardonnay

TO GARNISH

½ cup baby peas, steamed

4 asparagus tips, chopped

2 jarred roasted red peppers, cut into strips

1. Preheat the oven to 350°F. Place a large Dutch oven over medium heat; add half of the oil. Working in batches as needed, add the chicken, skin side down, and sear for 5 minutes. Flip the chicken and cook for an additional 5 minutes. Remove the chicken to a large casserole dish.

2. Next, add the remaining oil and sauté the onion, tomatoes, peppers, and garlic for 5 minutes. Pour the vegetable mixture over the chicken.

3. In the Dutch oven, add the chicken broth, rice, saffron, bay leaf, salt, and wine. Bring the mixture to a boil, then carefully pour the broth and rice mixture over the chicken in the casserole. Cover the casserole dish and bake for 20 to 25 minutes, or until the rice is tender and little moisture remains.

4. Garnish the casserole with the peas, asparagus, and roasted red peppers and serve.

DRY RUB RIBS

★ *Entertaining*

GRIFF JENKINS

**CORRESPONDENT,
FOX NEWS**

Having grown up in Tennessee, I'm no stranger to good barbecue. But in my hometown of Memphis, it was always the famed Rendezvous restaurant, run by the Vergos family, that was perhaps most well-known for spreading the love of dry rub ribs worldwide. Besides Elvis himself, dry rub barbecue is one of Memphis's most famous exports. While most pitmasters keep their recipes under lock and key, I'm more than happy to share what my wife, Kathleen, and daughters, Madeline and Mackenzie, love to devour. Although I've taken the time to put my own spin on the secret blend of dry herbs and spices, you could also have this rub sent via FedEx from the Rendezvous if you want the real thing—just don't expect to get *their* recipe! This dish is so special in our family, it's become the *traditional* go-to family meal on Christmas Eve. So, the rub will likely yield more than you will use for this recipe, but it can be stored in a dry, cool place to finish pork chops or barbecue chicken. Personally, I love to sprinkle some of it over hot scrambled eggs in the morning—you can thank me later! While most folks endorse a low and slow method when it comes to cooking ribs, I prefer to get my grill a bit hotter, cooking up the ribs over direct heat, while mopping them throughout the process in a sauce of more dry rub and vinegar. This grilled method turns out tender and meaty ribs that are ready to devour in just over an hour.

Serves 8

4 racks baby back ribs, membrane removed

¼ cup kosher salt

¼ cup fresh-cracked black pepper

Mop Sauce (recipe follows)

Finishing Rub (recipe follows)

1. Prepare the ribs by patting them dry and seasoning them liberally on both sides with kosher salt and fresh-cracked pepper.

2. Preheat a grill or smoker to medium heat. Arrange the ribs on the grate over direct heat, bone side down, and grill until sizzling and golden brown, 25 to 30 minutes. Turn the ribs and grill, meat side down, mopping with the sauce every 10 minutes, until sizzling and golden brown, for an additional 20 to 30 minutes.

3. To finish, mop the sauce over the ribs on both sides once more. Thickly sprinkle the meat with the finishing rub to form a crust. Slice the racks in half to serve.

MEET THE JENKINS!
FIRING UP THE GRILL W/ GRIFF & HIS FAMILY

THE FIVE @9PM ET

FOX NEWS channel

MOP SAUCE

1 cup distilled white vinegar

1 tablespoon kosher salt

2 tablespoons Finishing Rub
(recipe below)

Place 1 cup water, the vinegar, salt, and finishing rub in a small bowl and whisk until the salt is dissolved.

FINISHING RUB

3 tablespoons paprika

2 tablespoons chili powder

1 tablespoon kosher salt

2 teaspoons fresh-cracked black pepper

2 teaspoons garlic powder

2 teaspoons onion powder

2 teaspoons dried thyme

2 teaspoons dried oregano

2 teaspoons yellow mustard seeds

1 teaspoon ground coriander

1 teaspoon celery seed

½ teaspoon cayenne pepper

Place all of the ingredients in a small bowl and stir to mix.

DINER-STYLE BURGERS

CARLEY SHIMKUS

This quick at-home lunch rivals even your best diner-style burger. The key is to cook up the burgers in a skillet or pan to emulate that flat-top style from your favorite restaurant. In my opinion, your best friend here is a cast-iron skillet, as it heats evenly and gently, not to mention it's affordable and it lasts a lifetime. My favorite cast iron is made by Lodge right here in the USA. A little inside secret: you can actually stop in at their location in South Pittsburgh, Tennessee, to tour their museum of cast iron and the foundry, and do some shopping for a true taste of American-made. Cooking the burgers with this griddle-style method will ensure a nice crust to the burgers, while keeping them tender and cooking in their own juices for an even more flavorful result. While you can add whatever condiments you like, the finely chopped pickle and onion is my most treasured pick, especially when mixed with a mustard and mayo blend. American cheese is my go-to since it melts easily, but you can top your burger with any cheese that's to your liking. Good luck on having *just* one of these for lunch.

4 6-ounce hamburger patties

1 tablespoon kosher salt

1 tablespoon fresh-cracked black pepper

1½ teaspoons garlic powder

4 thick slices American cheese

Burger Sauce (recipe follows)

4 soft hamburger buns, warmed

1. Preheat a cast-iron skillet over medium heat. Meanwhile, generously season both sides of the patties with salt, pepper, and garlic powder. Add the patties to the skillet and cook for 3 to 4 minutes per side, or to desired doneness. In the final minute of cooking, top the burgers with the American cheese to melt just slightly.

2. To serve, spread the burger sauce on both halves of the cut buns. Place the burgers on the bottom portion of the bun and add the top bun. Serve immediately.

BURGER SAUCE

¼ cup mayonnaise

¼ cup yellow mustard

2 tablespoons finely chopped dill pickle

2 tablespoons finely chopped onion

Add all of the ingredients to a small bowl and stir until combined.

Chapter 3

APPETIZERS

CLAM DIP

MARTHA MACCALLUM

ANCHOR AND EXECUTIVE EDITOR,
THE STORY WITH
MARTHA MACCALLUM

An appetizer that will make any event flourish, this savory clam dip comes together as quickly as it's devoured. Since our family spends a lot of time on Cape Cod, this has become the go-to dish for an appetizer on Labor Day weekend, or as a side to a lobster supper. These kind of quick-fix recipes are especially helpful for me, since my schedule is always hectic. My secret? Canned clams are an affordable pantry staple, and they can be leveraged in this dish for a quick starter or folded into some cooked pasta for a speedy weeknight main. Clams (including the canned variety) boast plenty of protein, are low in fat, and contain minerals like iron and potassium that are essential to a healthy diet. The best part of this dish is that you can prep it several hours prior to your guests arriving, allowing the flavors to marry in the refrigerator until you're ready to serve. For best results, I recommend removing the cream cheese from the refrigerator to soften to make it easier to mix with the other ingredients—30 minutes or so will do the trick. If desired, a reduced-fat cream cheese and sour cream can be substituted to save a few calories. Serve this dish up with really anything that you can think of to dip into its savory, cheesy goodness; crackers or cut veggies are a classic.

1 8-ounce package cream cheese, softened at room temperature

6½ ounces canned minced clams, drained with 1 tablespoon clam juice reserved

¼ cup sour cream

½ teaspoon Worcestershire sauce

¼ teaspoon hot sauce

2 garlic cloves, minced

2 tablespoons minced fresh parsley

½ teaspoon ground black pepper

1 pinch of kosher salt

TO SERVE

Cut veggies

Assorted crackers

Add the cream cheese, reserved clam juice, sour cream, Worcestershire, and hot sauce and beat with an electric hand mixer until well combined. Stir in the clams, garlic, parsley, pepper, and salt. Serve with veggies and crackers.

Carley's Corner: There are only a few people I admire and look up to more than Martha. I will always remember that she was one of the first people who invited me to appear on her show as I began my own on-air journey. I will never forget that she took this chance and supported me.

ARTICHOKE PIE

★ *Family-Friendly* ★ *Cheap Eats* ★ *Comfort Food*

BRIAN KILMEADE
CO-HOST, *FOX & FRIENDS*

*M*y mother and her two sisters dominate all of the cooking in our family, especially around the holidays. A Kilmeade family favorite, this recipe was passed down from my mother to my daughters, Kristyn and Kaitlyn, as a comforting bite to start a meal, or to enjoy as a main dish rounded out with a fresh green salad. And now that my girls have been to grandma's "cooking school" I can count on the next generation of Kilmeades to keep this recipe alive. That's a sweet deal for me. Our secret ingredient is some meaty pepperoni—but a hard salami or soppressata can be substituted. If you want to skip the meat altogether, you can do that too for a vegetarian-friendly option. I prefer to use mozzarella grated by hand instead of the bagged version, as it melts better, creating a more decadent pie. Frozen piecrust dough is a time-saver that even Grandma endorses; use one disc to line the pie tin and the other to top the pie. If going the dinner route, this pie pairs nicely with a crisp sauvignon blanc or a warm, fruity zinfandel wine.

1 garlic clove, chopped

1 14-ounce can artichoke hearts, drained and quartered

1 tablespoon extra virgin olive oil

2 slices of pepperoni, diced

1 teaspoon kosher salt

1 teaspoon fresh-cracked black pepper

4 large eggs, beaten

2 cups grated mozzarella cheese

¼ cup grated Parmesan cheese

2 frozen piecrusts (about 14 ounces), such as Pillsbury Ready-to-Bake, thawed

1. Preheat the oven to 350°F. In a skillet over medium heat, sauté the garlic and artichoke hearts in the olive oil for 5 minutes. Transfer to a bowl, add the pepperoni, salt, pepper, and eggs and stir until blended. Add the mozzarella and Parmesan and stir to incorporate.

2. Line a 9-inch pie pan with one of the piecrusts and pour in the artichoke filling. Cover with the top crust, using your fingers to pinch the two crusts together to seal. Using a paring knife, cut a few slits in the top of the crust to vent.

3. Bake the pie until golden brown, approximately 45 minutes. Allow to cool for 30 minutes prior to serving.

Carley's Corner: I still find it crazy to believe that Brian, a host I watched during my childhood, is now a buddy of mine. Life has a funny way of being awesome. Brian and I met for the first time in 2011, while I was working on Fox Business Network as Don Imus's assistant. Our first conversation took place in the elevator bank (humble beginnings). I'm so fortunate to count Brian as both a colleague and friend.

GRILLED ANDOUILLE SAUSAGE

WITH CREOLE MUSTARD

★ *Entertaining* ★ *Cheap Eats*

CARLEY SHIMKUS

There's no better way to fire up a cookout than starting the party with this quick-and-easy appetizer. Dressing up a few store-bought ingredients by grilling and pairing is my quintessential entertainer's trick. It makes quick work look elegant for your guests. Andouille is a smoked pork sausage made most popular by Cajun cuisine, yet it can now be readily found in most grocery stores. It is one of my favorite varieties of sausage due to its versatility and kick, but in a pinch, any smoked pork sausage will do the trick. To keep it inspired by the bayou, I serve Creole mustard alongside as a tangy dipping sauce, but any whole-grain mustard can stand in its place. It's best to grill the sausages whole to keep them nice and juicy, then slice them on the bias just prior to serving. One more thing though: Pull a "me" move and be sure to take the first bite. It's for everyone's "safety," right? Once you've determined this app is 100 percent delicious, put it out to share with your friends.

1 pound Andouille sausage or other smoked pork sausage

2 tablespoons sliced green onions

½ cup Creole mustard or other whole-grain mustard

1. Prepare a two-zone charcoal fire over medium heat, or preheat a gas grill for 10 minutes with the dials set to medium heat on one side. Add the sausage to the grill over direct heat and cook on all sides until slightly charred, 2 to 3 minutes total. Transfer the sausage to indirect heat, cover the grill, and allow the sausage to cook through, an additional 5 to 7 minutes.

2. Remove the sausage to a cutting board and let rest for 3 to 5 minutes. Using a sharp knife, cut the sausage into ½-inch portions on the bias. Transfer the sliced sausage to a platter and garnish with the green onions. Add the mustard in a ramekin with toothpicks on the side so guests can serve themselves.

HUMMUS BOARD

★ *Entertaining* ★ *Healthy*

CARLEY SHIMKUS

It's a smorgas-board out there when it comes to all the fashionable ways of arranging your favorite ingredients for dipping and sharing on platters. But instead of trying to figure out which trend to follow next, I just like to dig in. After all, what could be better than a bit of hummus topped off with some crunchy and savory ingredients to invite your guests to demolish? Prepared hummus is a superfood store-bought ingredient that's packed with healthy fats and protein. This recipe calls for schmearing the goodness (hummus) all over a serving platter, followed by some favorite Greek-inspired ingredients to add a pop of flavor and color. Toasted pita chips make the perfect accompaniment, as their sturdy structure helps them carry the load. I've laid out one of my favorite versions for a hummus board, but feel free to follow your own inspiration here. This is a surefire winner that's eaten in as little time as it's prepared.

1 10-ounce container plain hummus

1 tablespoon finely chopped cucumber

1 tablespoon finely chopped tomato, preferably Roma

1 tablespoon finely chopped red onion

1 tablespoon finely chopped kalamata olives

2 tablespoons crumbled feta

1 tablespoon roughly chopped fresh dill fronds

1 tablespoon extra virgin olive oil

Pita chips, for serving

Scoop the hummus onto a serving platter and, using a rubber spatula, evenly spread the dip across the surface into a ⅛-inch-thick layer. Artfully top the hummus with the cucumber, tomato, onion, olives, and feta and garnish with the dill. Drizzle with the olive oil and serve with pita chips alongside.

TEX-MEX CHICKEN PULL-APART BREAD

★ *Entertaining* ★ *Comfort Food*

CHEF GEORGE DURAN

Not all breads are created equal; take for example this creative use of a store-bought loaf that's made into a starter, or a whole meal, frankly, by utilizing leftover rotisserie chicken and other kitchen staples. These kind of semi-homemade dishes are a cook's best friend, allowing you to take a few shortcuts when entertaining without sacrificing any flavor. This particular appetizer is a great choice for your next cookout, as it brings everything together over indirect heat on your grill. But don't worry, if the grill is not fired up, you can pull this off in your oven. Score the bread in a grid-like pattern to create your own pull-apart pieces and fill all of the nooks and crannies with the chicken, cheese, and salsa trifecta. My advice? Don't skimp when it comes to choosing the salsa because it's the dipping sauce that brings this dish together. Source a fresh-cut salsa—found in the refrigerator case instead of a jar—for best results. When it's time to devour, really get in there and invite your guests to do the same, grabbing and pulling bites with one hand, and using the other hand to catch any bites that might fall while making their way into your mouths. Don't be shy on this one, you can wash that stained T-shirt tomorrow!

Serves 6

1 12-inch crusty round bread loaf

1 cup store-bought pulled rotisserie chicken

8 tablespoons (1 stick) unsalted butter, melted

1 1-ounce packet taco seasoning mix

1 cup grated mozzarella cheese

1 cup grated Monterey Jack cheese

1 16-ounce container fresh salsa, such as Fresh Cravings, plus more for dipping

1. Preheat one side of a gas grill to medium heat, or preheat your oven to 350°F. Using a bread knife, score the top of the bread loaf into a grid-like pattern, cutting about three-quarters of the way into the bread, but taking care to leave the base intact.

2. Mix the rotisserie chicken with the melted butter, taco seasoning, cheeses, and salsa. Using your fingers or a spoon, carefully disperse the chicken mixture in between the slits in the bread.

3. Securely wrap the loaf with its filling in foil. Place on the grill rack over indirect heat and bake for 15 minutes. Next, remove the foil from the top of the loaf and continue to bake until the topping is bubbly, 5 to 10 minutes. Serve the pull-apart bread on a platter with additional salsa on the side.

BBQ DEVILED EGGS

★ *Entertaining*

CARLEY SHIMKUS

No barbecue is complete without some deviled eggs. But, instead of having to wait for a barbecue to get your fix, this recipe combines the two concepts for a new classic to get the meal started. To make your life easy, I suggest picking up store-bought pulled pork (or even better, pork sourced from your favorite barbecue joint); it's folded into the yolk mixture that fills the deviled eggs for a meaty surprise. You can also substitute chopped brisket or sausage. (I rarely have any leftovers lying around after a Saturday smoke!) After that, the filled eggs are topped with a dry rub. Pick this up at the market or make your own; either way, it will get your taste buds ready for the main course. I always recommend making hard-boiled eggs from eggs that were purchased several days before—fresh eggs are a touch harder to peel. If you are short on time, you can thankfully now buy already hard-boiled, peeled eggs, which makes this a last-minute friendly appetizer to serve without the stress.

12 large eggs

½ cup mayonnaise, preferably Duke's

1 tablespoon yellow mustard

1 tablespoon very finely chopped dill pickle

½ teaspoon kosher salt

½ teaspoon fresh-cracked black pepper

1 splash of hot sauce

¼ cup finely chopped smoked pork

TO FINISH

About 1 teaspoon dry rub

1 teaspoon finely sliced chives

1. In a large pan, arrange the eggs into a single layer and submerge under water, covering them by at least 1 inch when measured from the top. Bring eggs to a boil over medium-high heat, turn off the heat (leaving the pan on the burner), cover, and allow the eggs to sit for 10 minutes. Remove the eggs to an ice bath until cooled, about 5 minutes. To peel, tap the eggs on a flat hard surface and remove the shells under cold running water.

2. Slice eggs lengthwise and, using a spoon, very carefully remove the egg yolks to a medium-size mixing bowl. Transfer the egg whites to a serving platter. Add the mayonnaise, mustard, pickle, salt, pepper, and hot sauce to the yolks and mash with a fork until evenly combined. Next, fold the pork into the yolk mixture until combined.

3. Spoon the yolk mixture evenly into the egg white halves. Garnish with a sprinkle of the dry rub and the chives. Serve.

HERB AND GARLIC BUTTER BOARD

★ *Entertaining*

CARLEY SHIMKUS

There's now a new kid in town when it comes to serving bread and butter. The viral butter board trend is here to stay (splendid, because who can't get enough bread and butter?), and it offers an artist's canvas of fun and exciting opportunities to amp up this traditional pairing. The key here is to use the best butter possible; local or European varieties are typically rich in flavor. While unsalted butter is most often used for cooking (it allows you to control the salt input of your dish), lightly salted butter is your best friend for this presentation. The butter board is a choose-your-own-adventure kind of experience, but my personal favorite combines the butter with fresh herbs and garlic for an exciting twist on garlic bread. Fortunately for us, the technique couldn't be more simple. Lay the butter out at room temperature at least 30 minutes prior to spreading the board, then top with your favorite ingredients. I do like to use a marble or stone board that's been chilled in the fridge to help the butter maintain the right consistency. Sliced crusty bread rounds or crackers can be served alongside to enjoy.

8 tablespoons (1 stick) good-quality salted butter, softened at room temperature

1 teaspoon lemon zest

1 head garlic, peeled and finely minced

1 teaspoon finely chopped chives

1 teaspoon crushed red pepper

10 leaves fresh basil

¼ teaspoon fleur de sel, or flaky salt

1 tablespoon extra virgin olive oil

Sliced French bread rounds, to serve

On a serving platter, use a rubber spatula to evenly spread the butter over the platter in an approximately ⅛-inch-thick layer. Next, artfully arrange the lemon zest, garlic, chives, red pepper flakes, and basil leaves evenly on top of the butter. Season with the salt and drizzle with the olive oil. Serve the sliced bread rounds alongside the garlic butter.

MEAT AND CHEESE PLATE

★ *Entertaining*

CARLEY SHIMKUS

Nowadays, charcuterie platters are an essential starter at restaurants or home dinners. But giving the fancy name (charcuterie) isn't necessary, as meat and cheese plates have long been a staple, especially in America's heartland. Whatever you call it, the combination of cured meats, cheeses, and pickled vegetables (and, frankly, anything else you want to add to the platter) is a great starter or even a meal. I like to tell folks that they don't need to limit their creativity when they're enjoying one of these platters. Encourage each of your guests to build their own perfect bite by arranging a few types of meats, cheeses, and other delights that inspire them. If you have access to a specialty cheese shop, they can help guide you in your decision-making as you build your platter. After all, there are thousands of varieties and combinations out there—why not get some help from the experts? That said, don't feel pressured to get too complicated, or expensive for that matter. A meat and cheese board is meant to be a laissez-faire appetizer that pairs well with all varieties of wine, beer, cocktails, and, *of course*, friends.

On a serving platter, artfully arrange the ingredients as desired. Garnish with fresh herbs and serve alongside assorted crackers and toast.

4 ounces thinly sliced aged Asiago cheese

6 ounces cubed Jack cheese

6 ounces cubed sharp cheddar cheese

1 4-ounce log herbed goat cheese

1 small round Brie cheese

4 ounces thinly sliced prosciutto cotto or branded ham

4 ounces thinly sliced capicola

2 ounces thinly sliced pepperoni

4 ounces thinly sliced soppressata

4 ounces hard salami, cut into cubes

1 cup assorted pitted olives

1 cup cornichons

1 cup fresh blueberries (or blackberries)

1 cup fresh raspberries

1 cup dried plums

Fresh herbs, such as rosemary, chive, and thyme, for garnish

Assorted crackers and toasted bread rounds, for serving

BEER BRAT SLIDERS WITH MUSTARD

★ *Entertaining* ★ *Cheap Eats*

CHEF MATT MOORE

'll be the first to admit, I'm no gridiron great, save for maybe my high school state championship title. And while I've got some cooking cred these days, it's actually my wife, Callie Stydahar Moore, who comes from NFL royalty. After all, her grandfather Joe Stydahar was not only the Chicago Bears' first draft pick ever, but he is also in the NFL Hall of Fame. On top of his success as a player, Stydahar served as head coach of the Los Angeles Rams, ushering them to the world championship in the 1950s. But Callie will share that I have other talents, including my "love language" of cooking and sharing food. So, to share the love, I concocted this beer brat slider recipe for Callie to celebrate and recognize her home state of Wisconsin. Ain't nothing wrong with cooking up a little romance in the kitchen too! This recipe calls for a two-step method of cooking the brats, in a beer and onion mixture first, followed by a sear that ensures they are cooked perfectly, charred and juicy.

1 large sweet onion, thinly sliced

3 thyme sprigs

1 12-ounce bottle pale ale, such as Sierra Nevada

2 tablespoons course-grained mustard, plus more for serving

2 tablespoons apple cider vinegar

1 tablespoon honey

1 teaspoon kosher salt

3 4-ounce bratwurst links

6 2-ounce mini-hoagie rolls, such as King's Hawaiian

1. Stir together the onion, thyme, beer, mustard, vinegar, honey, and salt in a cast-iron skillet. Submerge the bratwurst links and let them marinate while you prepare the grill.

2. Open the bottom and top vents of a charcoal grill completely. Light a charcoal chimney starter filled halfway with charcoal. When the coals are covered with gray ash, pour them onto the bottom grate of the grill. Adjust the vents as needed to maintain an internal temperature of 400°F. If using a gas grill, preheat to medium-high.

3. Place the skillet with the bratwurst mixture on unoiled grates in the center of the grill. Grill, covered, until the bratwursts are cooked through, about 30 minutes.

4. Remove the bratwursts to a platter and set aside. Move the skillet to the perimeter of the grill and cook the onion mixture, uncovered, stirring occasionally, until the mixture thickens into a relish, about 20 minutes. Remove from the heat and discard the thyme.

5. While the onion mixture cooks, place the bratwursts directly on oiled grates. Grill, uncovered, turning occasionally until browned and crisp, about 10 minutes. Transfer to a cutting board and let cool slightly, about 5 minutes. Slice each bratwurst in half crosswise at an angle.

6. Spoon 2 tablespoons of the onion relish into each split roll; top with half a bratwurst and a dollop of mustard. Arrange the brats on a serving platter.

Chapter 4

DINNER

LINGUINE WITH CLAM SAUCE

ED SHIMKUS
MY FATHER

Because I was brought up in a Lithuanian household, you wouldn't think I would highlight this dish (which primarily traces its roots to Italian cuisine) as a favorite, but it is. And while I have sampled this particular dish at many restaurants over the years, and most versions were very good, there was something missing. Sometimes, if you want something done right, you do it yourself! So, one day I went about making my own version of this beloved classic and I discovered the missing flavor I craved by emphasizing the basics of the dish. In my version, the dish went from good to great when I focused on using fresh clams only, and plenty of fresh garlic as well. It's a simple recipe, and to make your life a bit easier, you can prepare the time-consuming parts like shucking the clams and peeling the garlic ahead of time. I like to serve this alongside a green salad to round out the meal. So here it goes. I hope you enjoy it as much as Carley, my wife, Zulma, and Carley's sister, Margot.

1 dozen live cherrystone or chowder clams

1 head of fresh garlic

1 tablespoon kosher salt

1 pound linguine

4 to 6 ounces extra virgin olive oil

4 8-ounce bottles clam juice

2 tablespoons chopped fresh parsley leaves

1. Place the clams in a large pot or bowl and fill with hot tap water. Change the water several times, or until the clams begin to open. Using a paring knife, carefully remove the clams from their shells and place them in another bowl, reserving all of their liquid.

2. Next, cut the clams with kitchen scissors into small pieces, about ¼ to ½ inches. If desired, the clams can be shucked and cut ahead of time and kept covered in the refrigerator for up to 12 hours prior to cooking.

3. Peel the entire head of garlic, separate all of the cloves, and peel each clove. Using a knife, trim the ends from the garlic cloves and slice each clove into thin slivers.

4. Meanwhile, pour approximately 12 cups of water into a 6-quart pot, add the salt, and bring to a boil over high heat. Cook the pasta, stirring on occasion, for exactly 8 minutes.

5. While the pasta is cooking, add the oil to a 4-quart pot over medium heat, add the garlic slices and fry until slightly brown, about 1 minute, taking care that the garlic doesn't burn. Remove the pan from the heat and, using a slotted spoon, remove and discard the garlic. When the garlic oil has cooled, add the clam juice, reserved sliced clams with their juices, and the parsley to the pot. Return the pot to medium-high heat, bring to a boil, and quickly remove from the heat.

6. When pasta has finished cooking, drain off approximately three-fourths of the cooking water, reserving the rest of the pasta water in the pot with the linguine. Pour the clam sauce into the pasta, using a slotted spoon to hold back the clam pieces, and stir until well combined. Ladle the pasta and clam sauce into serving bowls, spoon the clam pieces on top of the pasta, and serve.

CORNED BEEF
WITH RICE AND BEANS

ZULMA SHIMKUS
MY MOTHER

Rice and beans is a staple dish that reflects my Puerto Rican heritage, and it's something I passed on to my daughters as a traditional family favorite. To add variety, stewed meats seasoned with sofrito, thinly sliced marinated steak (bistec), or roasted meats such as the classic pernil asado (a roasted ham shoulder seasoned with salt, garlic, and black pepper) are typically served alongside the rice and beans. That said, rice and beans can stand on their own too for a hearty meal any time of the year. For Carley and her sister, Margot, there was a constant rotation of different meats to go with rice and beans. Yet, despite all of the variety these delicious choices provided, Carley often craved canned corned beef served with white rice and beans, especially during her pregnancy. Making use of the canned corned beef is a real time-saver, and when cooked in a quick tomato sauce and topped with poached eggs, it is a true comfort-food dish.

2 tablespoons extra virgin olive oil

2 12-ounce cans corned beef

6 to 8 ounces canned tomato sauce

4 large eggs

Rice and Beans (recipe follows)

1. Heat the oil in a large skillet over medium-low heat until warm. Next, remove the corned beef from the cans, scraping off any fat that coats the meat, and add the meat to the pan. Using a spoon, break the corned beef into smaller chunks and cook until the meat is thoroughly heated and the chunks are broken down in the oil.

2. Add the tomato sauce and stir to combine, cooking for 1 minute and stirring often to warm it. Working with one egg at a time, make small openings in the meat mixture and drop a cracked egg in each opening. Break the yolks if desired. Cook the eggs for 2 minutes, allowing them to set. Stir the mixture gently a few times, or until eggs are cooked. Serve the corned beef mixture alongside rice and beans.

RICE AND BEANS

ZULMA SHIMKUS
MY MOTHER

I will always be grateful to my aunt Elsie Olga Alvarado, or Titi Olga, as we call her, because she helped me work out the quantities for my mom's recipes, a difficult job, especially since none of us in our family use conventional measuring cups and spoons. While you can use any variety of rice you prefer, white rice, in my opinion, is most traditional. The rice that sticks to the bottom of the pot is no mistake. In fact, it has its own name, *pegau*, which is a variation of the Spanish word pegado, meaning "stuck" in English, and my family loves it. Eat it carefully though, if you decide to try it, because pegau can be very hard. If you have trouble removing the pegau from your pot, just add a bit of water to it and simmer for 5 to 10 minutes to release it. Carley's grandmother Margot Aponte traditionally used dried beans and simmered them until tender before using them in her rice and bean recipe. Today, many cooks, including me, use canned beans because it's quick and convenient. A very important ingredient in Puerto Rican cooking is sofrito, a paste of onions, peppers, and tomato with different herbs, that is at the core of the delicious and unique flavor of many of our dishes. When time permits, I pick up specialty ingredients online or at a Hispanic market, then I make a batch of sofrito and freeze it in containers to use throughout the year. If pressed for time, I follow Titi Olga's shortcut of using Goya's frozen sofrito (it comes in a blue-and-white container). Instead of using olives, as is called for in my version, Titi Olga adds two to three pieces of cured meat to the beans in the final 10 minutes or so for an added twist. Also, if desired you can add cut pieces of either calabaza squash or potatoes to the beans along with about half a cup of water in the last 15 to 20 minutes, cooking them until tender.

BEANS

1 tablespoon extra virgin olive oil

¼ cup sofrito, preferably Goya

4 tablespoons tomato sauce

12 to 15 pimiento-stuffed Spanish olives

1 heaping teaspoon of nonpareil capers

1 pinch of kosher salt

2 15.5-ounce cans beans, pink, pinto, great northern, navy, or your choice

Rice (recipe follows)

1. In a Dutch oven over medium-high heat, add the oil followed by the sofrito and sauté for 2 minutes. Add the tomato sauce and continue to sauté the sofrito for another 2 minutes. Next, add the olives, capers, salt, and canned beans with their juices and stir to combine. Pour a bit of water into both of the empty bean cans, about ¼ cup, swirl the water in the cans, and add to the Dutch oven.

2. Bring the mixture to a gentle boil and cook, uncovered, for 5 minutes, stirring often. Reduce the heat to low, partially cover the pot, and simmer the beans for 15 minutes. Remove from the heat and serve the beans and sauce over cooked rice.

RICE

3 cups medium-grain white rice, preferably Goya

4 tablespoons extra virgin olive oil

1½ teaspoons kosher salt

1. Rinse the rice according to package instructions, removing and discarding any blemished grains.

2. In a heavy-bottomed 3-quart pot over medium-high heat, add the rice, oil, and salt and sauté the rice, stirring often, for 2 minutes. Remove the rice from the heat and let cool down for 1 minute. Next, add 3½ cups of water, return the pot to the heat, and bring to a boil, stirring often. Reduce the heat to medium-low and simmer, stirring to keep the rice from sticking to the bottom of the pot too early in the cooking process. Continue to simmer until the rice is exposed and most of the water has been absorbed. Reduce the heat to low, stir, and cover with the lid.

3. Cook the rice, covered and uninterrupted for 25 to 30 minutes. When ready to serve, uncover and fluff the rice with a fork.

SEMI-HOMEMADE POT PIE

★ *Family-Friendly* ★ *Cheap Eats* ★ *Comfort Food*

SHANNON BREAM
ANCHOR, *FOX NEWS SUNDAY*

When it comes to cooking anything, I like to say that all is fair in love and the kitchen. After all, that's my kind of blasé culinary approach. After a busy workday, getting a homemade dinner on the table can be a challenge. It's a conundrum that I know all too well because of my busy hosting and reporting schedule. Though I'm first to admit cooking is not my strong suit, instead of dialing for takeout, I solve the dinner problem by using a few store-bought shortcuts to pull off this meal. This comforting chicken pot pie might include a few time-savers—I rarely make anything that's completely homemade—but there's no sacrifice on the flavor. Besides, when it comes out of the oven with that beautiful crust, people will think you went through a lot more effort to make this than you actually did. Even better yet, most of these ingredients can be stored in your pantry or freezer for the next time the dinner bell rings or hunger strikes. In less than an hour, with little to no prep, you can enjoy a family meal around the table without breaking the bank. For a change of pace, I also like to substitute canned tuna for the canned chicken for another savory twist.

1 14.5-ounce can mixed vegetables (green beans, carrots, corn, potatoes), drained

1 12.5 ounce can white chunk chicken, drained

2 10.5-ounce cans cream of potato soup

Splash of whole milk

½ teaspoon dried oregano

½ teaspoon kosher salt

½ teaspoon fresh-cracked black pepper

2 frozen piecrusts (about 14 ounces), such as Pillsbury Ready-to-Bake, thawed

1. Preheat the oven to 375°F. Next, mix together the vegetables, chicken, soup, milk, oregano, salt, and pepper in a bowl.

2. Line a 9-inch pie pan with one layer of the pie crust dough. Pour the soup mixture into the pan, and top with a second layer of pie crust dough, using your fingers to press together and seal the crusts. Use a paring knife to cut a few slits in the top of the pie to vent.

3. Bake in the preheated oven for 45 minutes, or until the piecrust is golden brown. Let cool for 15 to 20 minutes prior to serving.

CHICKEN POT PIE
POTATO SOUP, CANNED VEGGIES MAKE UP FILLING

FOX NEWS channel

FOX & friends

LINGUINE WITH CORN, ASPARAGUS, AND LEEKS

JESSICA TARLOV
CO-HOST, *THE FIVE*

*W*hen I'm not dishing up politics on air, I love cooking up this delicious dish with my family. Cooking is personal for me, and this recipe hails from my father, Mark Tarlov, a former filmmaker who attended evening culinary school, an extra creative hobby, while working at the Department of Justice. Dad was always up to something, and he created this pasta to feed us something foolproof. It's a comfort meal that always brings back fond memories of Dad's presence. One piece of advice: Don't let the veggie-laden recipe title fool you—this dish highlights a delicious base of bacon that asserts its smoky, meaty flavor throughout the vegetable-laced pasta. And if you've never cooked with leeks, have no fear, as these friends from the onion family will become your new go-to; just be sure to thoroughly rinse them under cold running water to remove any sand or grit after procuring them from the market or grocery store. A one-pan dish, this is a hearty pasta that's also light enough to enjoy on a summer night. To add some heft, you could top it with a nicely seared piece of fish or sautéed shrimp. Serve this as a main alongside a green salad and warmed bread to keep it fresh. And to top it off, pair with a crisp sauvignon blanc or un-oaked chardonnay to elevate this to an extra-special dinner to share.

2 teaspoons kosher salt

24 ounces dried linguine

4 ounces hardwood-smoked bacon, roughly diced into chunks

3 ears fresh corn, kernels cut from the cob

7 spears fresh asparagus, ends trimmed and cut into 1-inch pieces

2 leeks, washed (see headnote) and cut into ¼-inch matchsticks

¼ cup extra virgin olive oil, plus more for finishing

4 tablespoons (½ stick) unsalted butter

FOR SERVING

¼ cup finely minced chives

Fresh-cracked black pepper

6 ounces Parmesan cheese, grated

1. Bring a large stockpot filled with water to a boil over medium-high heat; add 1 teaspoon of the salt. Add the linguine and cook to al dente per package instructions.

2. Meanwhile, add the bacon to a large sauté pan over medium heat. Cook the bacon, stirring on occasion, until crispy and brown, 6 to 7 minutes. Use a slotted spoon to transfer the bacon to a paper towel–lined plate and increase the heat for the pan to medium-high. Next, add the corn, asparagus, leeks, and olive oil to the pan and sauté until the vegetables are tender, 5 to 7 minutes. As the pasta finishes cooking, add some of the pasta water (about ¼ to ½ cup) to the vegetables. Add the butter and melt, adding more pasta water to thin the sauce as desired.

3. To finish, add the bacon to the sauté pan followed by the pasta. Using tongs, toss the pasta in the sauce and vegetable mixture, adding a drizzle of olive oil if desired. Transfer the pasta to a platter and top with the chives, fresh-cracked pepper, and grated Parmesan cheese. Serve.

Carley's Corner: **When I first discovered I would become a mom, I had a lot of hesitations. Like, I had never even changed a diaper before. Would I be a good mom? How would I balance work and motherhood? It turns out, my anxiety over this change was normal, and Jessica has been my rock for all things, from advice to just being a friend to rely on throughout this stage of my life. One of the reasons I love working at FOX is because I'm surrounded by sweet and smart folks like Jessica.**

THAI SHRIMP WITH GARLIC

★ *Family-Friendly* ★ *Healthy* ★ *Entertaining*

DANIEL HOFFMAN
CONTRIBUTOR, FOX NEWS

During my time as a former station chief with the CIA, I was fortunate to see my fair share of the world. And while I might not be at liberty to discuss all of my assignments and travels, you can assume I've eaten my way around the world a few times! My late wife, Kim, would have been be the first to tell you, "It's been a crazy life, but a good one." My favorite part is that this Thai-inspired shrimp dish will transport me and anyone who makes it to Thailand in an instant, without having to leave home. The key here is to source the freshest shrimp possible; splurge on the best quality you can find since the rest of the ingredients are relatively inexpensive. Fortunately, these days you can pick up the majority of these Thai and Asian ingredients in the specialty aisle of your local supermarket.

Ironically, I actually picked up this recipe from a Thai restaurant in Finland, of all places, when I was studying Finnish. On the last night of my stay, the kind folks at this restaurant gave me a book with recipes, including this inspiration. Study up I did, and this dish became one of the first that I cooked for Kim when we were dating. I knew she was a keeper, because like me, we both shared a love for garlic. While I don't make promises I can't keep, a loving marriage and two kids are the proving ground that this recipe will likely become one of your favorites too.

Serves 4

¼ cup vegetable oil

4 garlic cloves, finely chopped

½ pound large shrimp, peeled and deveined

¼ cup Thai coconut milk

¼ cup sliced button mushrooms

¼ teaspoon fresh-cracked black pepper

2 teaspoons fish sauce

2 teaspoons brown sugar

½ cup green Thai chili paste

3 cups very finely chopped cabbage

4 cups cooked jasmine rice, kept warm for serving

1. In a large skillet or wok, heat the oil over medium-high heat. Add the garlic and stir-fry for 30 seconds, or until lightly browned. Next, add the shrimp, coconut milk, mushrooms, pepper, fish sauce, brown sugar, and chili paste. Cook, stirring constantly, for 8 to 10 minutes, or until the shrimp are bright pink and firm.

2. To serve, line a platter with the warm rice and top with the sliced cabbage and shrimp stir-fry and plenty of the coconut milk sauce.

SPAGHETTI SQUASH AND CHICKEN MEATBALLS

★ *Family-Friendly* ★ *Healthy*

CHEF COLLINS WOODS
&
JOHNNY JOEY JONES

CONTRIBUTOR, FOX NEWS

In my service to my country, I spent most of my time working as a chief bomb technician in the Marines. These days, I like to continue to give back, serving up this delicious meal alongside my pal Collins Woods, who is the executive chef at Camp Southern Ground—a summer camp founded by country musician Zac Brown with a special focus on military kids and their families. The camp and its mission are personal to me, so it was a no-brainer to get involved after retiring from the military. This dish is a healthy spin on a tasty classic, spaghetti and meatballs. By using spaghetti squash "noodles," instead of pasta, it offers a low-carb, gluten-free alternative that lightens up the dish. Chef Woods's technique of roasting the squash over high heat ensures that it will release most of its moisture while cooking, making for the perfect spaghetti-like texture. That said, if you are craving the real thing, feel free to cook up some spaghetti too. From there, the savory chicken meatballs add some satisfying heft to the dish and keep the kiddos asking for second helpings. Most important, this is my kids' favorite meal—and that's what it's all about. Oh, and bonus points for serving this dish in the squash shells, which means no dishes to clean up after dinner!

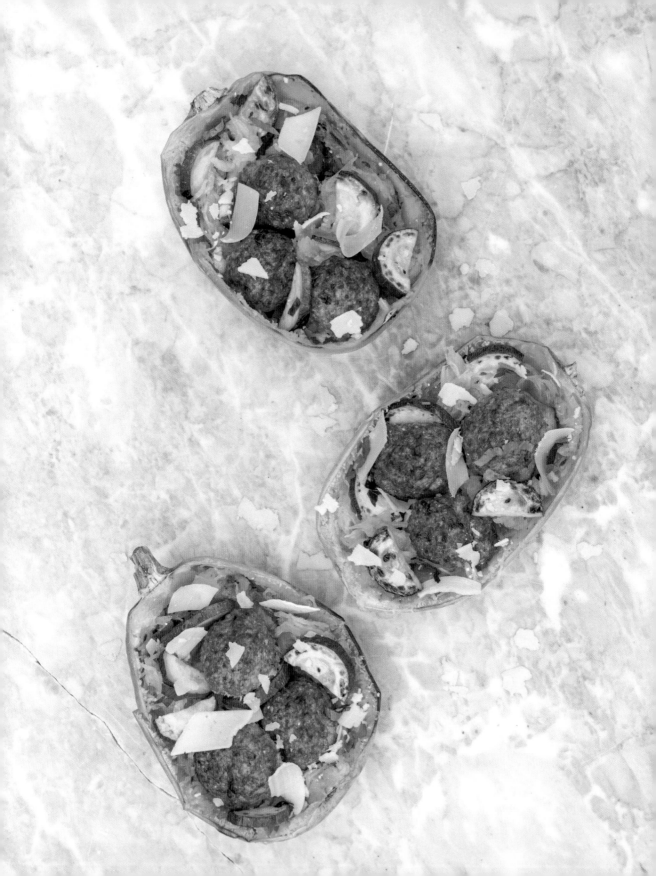

Serves 4

SQUASH

2 small or medium spaghetti squash (about 8 pounds total)

Kosher salt

Fresh-cracked black pepper

6 tablespoons unsalted butter

2 small zucchini, sliced lengthwise and cut into ½-inch half-moons

1 teaspoon granulated garlic

1 cup roughly chopped fresh parsley

1 cup shaved Parmesan cheese

1 cup shaved Asiago cheese

1 cup shaved pecorino cheese

MEATBALLS

1 pound ground chicken

1 pound ground turkey

1 cup gluten-free bread crumbs

2 tablespoons finely chopped fresh parsley

2 tablespoons finely chopped fresh tarragon

4 garlic cloves, minced

½ cup minced onion

1 cup grated pecorino cheese

1 tablespoon ground fennel

2 large eggs, beaten

Grated zest of 1 lemon

Kosher salt

Fresh-cracked black pepper

1. Preheat the oven to 400°F. Carefully, with a large sharp knife, cut the squashes in half lengthwise, creating 4 halves. Using a spoon, scoop out and discard the seeds from each half. Next, season the squash halves with the salt and pepper to taste. Place them flesh side down on a baking sheet and roast for 45 to 50 minutes.

2. Let the squash rest for 10 to 15 minutes. When cool to the touch, use a fork to scrape out the flesh in strands, reserving the shells for later use.

3. Meanwhile, prepare the meatballs by mixing all of the meatball ingredients together in a large bowl and seasoning with the salt and pepper to taste. Using your hands, form meatballs, each approximately 2 ounces or about 1½ inches in diameter, and place on a baking sheet, being careful not to crowd them. Bake the meatballs until browned and cooked through, approximately 12 minutes.

4. To finish, melt the butter in a large skillet over medium-low heat. Add the zucchini and sauté for 2 to 3 minutes. Reduce the heat to low, add the reserved spaghetti squash, the garlic, and half of the parsley mixture. Add the meatballs straight from the oven to the pan, along with half of each of the grated cheeses. Toss for 1 to 2 minutes, or until the cheese melts into the sauce.

5. To serve, spoon the meatballs, squash noodles, and sauce into the squash shells, and top with cheeses and parsley.

GUY'S MUSTARD-ENCRUSTED SALMON

★ *Healthy*

GUY BENSON

HOST, THE GUY BENSON SHOW, FOX NEWS RADIO

I have no shame in admitting that I'm not the most habitual home cook, but this delicious salmon is actually a recipe I developed during my time working as a host at a small restaurant in Ridgewood, New Jersey. Sometimes, even if you don't work in a kitchen, a few restaurant secrets make their way into your repertoire. Such is the case with this delicious meal that I reverse engineered after leaving the restaurant so I could still get that satisfying meal I craved. This is a recipe that I cook for myself all the time. It's very easy to make, easy to clean up, and it's quick, which is important for me. Salmon makes for a great protein to incorporate into your diet weekly, as it's loaded with omega-3 fats that support a healthy lifestyle. Rounded out with some quick-cooking garlicky spinach and a caprese salad, this is a healthy supper you can rely on when time and convenience are equally important as a delicious meal.

4 tablespoons mayonnaise, preferably Duke's

1 tablespoon Dijon mustard

2 tablespoons grated Parmesan cheese

2 6- to 8-ounce salmon fillets

2 tablespoons extra virgin olive oil

1 garlic clove, minced

4 cups loosely packed fresh spinach

1 cup grape tomatoes

¼ teaspoon kosher salt

¼ teaspoon fresh-cracked black pepper

1. Preheat the oven to 380°F. In a small bowl, mix together the mayonnaise, mustard, and Parmesan. Put the salmon fillets on a sheet pan and brush them with the sauce. Bake for 15 to 20 minutes, or until slightly firm to the touch.

2. Meanwhile, add 1 tablespoon of the extra virgin olive oil to a large skillet over medium heat. Next, add the garlic and cook for 30 seconds. Add the spinach, toss with the garlic, and sauté until just wilted, 45 to 60 seconds.

3. Drain any excess water from the spinach and evenly divide the spinach between two dinner plates. Top with the salmon. In a small bowl, combine the tomatoes, mozzarella, the remaining 1 tablespoon olive oil, and the salt and pepper and toss to mix. Plate the tomato and mozzarella salad next to the salmon fillets and serve.

SPINACH AND MUSHROOM LASAGNA

★ *Healthy* ★ *Family-Friendly*

DR. NICOLE SAPHIER
CONTRIBUTOR, FOX NEWS

As a medical expert, I also love to cook, especially foods that promote overall wellness. Family recipes are part of the healthy makeover, and I like to put a spin on my grandmother's (ma-mom's) famous lasagna by layering in spinach and mushrooms instead of meat. Mushrooms pack a punch of protein without the fat and extra calories found in meat. Making small substitutions like this on a weekly basis can help you reach your health goals, without sacrificing that comfort food craving. I've devoted my entire medical career to helping those, like my grandmother, who have been diagnosed with breast cancer, and a healthy lifestyle is something I endorse as part of an overall plan for wellness. That said, I made a few adjustments to this recipe that my ma-mom wouldn't approve of, like using oven-ready lasagna noodles, a big time-saver that makes this a weeknight-friendly meal for working moms and dads. But whether she approved or not, I know she would love the fact that I'm still in the kitchen doing what we loved to do together. If you've never used these oven-ready noodles, just make sure they are completely submerged in the sauce to ensure they cook perfectly. When it comes to assembling the lasagna, don't worry about making it nice and neat; it's all going to melt at some point, and putting some toothpicks on the cheesy top prevents the foil from sticking to it. This delicious and healthy vegetarian-friendly recipe can serve as a comforting meal during the week without the guilt.

1 garlic clove, sliced

1 teaspoon extra virgin olive oil, plus more for greasing the pan

1 8-ounce package sliced mushrooms

1 10-ounce bag fresh spinach

2 pounds whole-milk ricotta cheese

1 8-ounce bag shredded mozzarella cheese

1 large egg

1 cup grated Parmesan cheese

1 teaspoon garlic powder

½ teaspoon kosher salt

½ teaspoon fresh-cracked black pepper

1 pinch of crushed red pepper flakes

1 24-ounce jar tomato sauce, such as Classico

1 9- to 12-ounce box oven-ready lasagna noodles

8 ounces sliced fresh mozzarella cheese, such as BelGioioso

1 cup grated pecorino cheese

1. Preheat the oven to 375°F. In a large sauté pan over medium heat, add the garlic and oil and cook for 30 seconds. Next, add the mushrooms and sauté them for 60 seconds. Add the spinach and stir and cook the mixture until the spinach is wilted, 1 to 2 minutes. Drain the liquid from the pan and set aside.

2. In a large bowl, mix together the ricotta, shredded mozzarella, egg, Parmesan, garlic powder, salt, pepper, and red pepper flakes. Add the drained spinach mixture to the cheese and stir until well combined.

3. Grease a 9 × 13-inch casserole dish with olive oil. Next, add a thin layer of tomato sauce in the bottom of the casserole. Place a single layer of oven-ready lasagna noodles on top of the sauce. Add another thin layer of tomato sauce followed by a thick layer of the cheese-spinach filling. Repeat layering the lasagna noodles, tomato sauce, and cheese-spinach filling. To finish, add one more layer of lasagna noodles, a layer of tomato sauce, and top with the fresh mozzarella slices and pecorino cheese.

4. Place toothpicks in the corners of the baking dish, and cover the dish with heavy-duty aluminum foil, being careful not to allow the toothpicks to puncture the foil. Bake for 25 minutes. Remove the foil and bake for another 10 to 15 minutes. Let rest for 10 minutes before serving.

NOTE: For an impressive finish, you can broil the cheese under the broiler, set to high, for 2 minutes, or until the cheese is golden brown. Fresh chopped parsley can be used to garnish.

RIGATONI Á LA BOLOGNESE

★ *Comfort Food* ★ *Entertaining*

CARLEY SHIMKUS

Pasta and meat sauce, there is perhaps nothing more comforting and satisfying than this centuries-old combination. Bolognese sauce is a red, tomato- and wine-based braise that is cooked low and slow for several hours, usually with an array of proteins, and served over hot cooked pasta. For this recipe, I like rigatoni, as its larger shape provides a big meaty bite, but perhaps the best part is the ridges of the pasta, and of course the tubular shape, which gets filled with sauce, packing each bite with a punch of flavor. I'll go ahead and forewarn you—this recipe calls for a full bottle of red wine; of course you can have a glass for yourself if desired, but the wine is key to this dish. You don't need to open up your vintage varietals for this recipe; a casual, drinking wine that you would enjoy on a weeknight will do the trick. As the bolognese cooks, the flavor of the wine will reduce; initially it will taste a bit sour, but after a few hours of cooking, it will produce a warm, rich sauce. My preferred meat combination is beef and pork, but adding veal, sausage, or wild game to this sauce is totally cool too. Fresh grated Parmesan cheese and a hearty red (more wine is always celebrated) is all you need to enjoy this dish as a comforting meal.

1 pound 80/20 ground beef

1 pound ground pork sausage

1 teaspoon kosher salt

1 teaspoon fresh-cracked black pepper

1 teaspoon ground cinnamon

1 cup finely minced yellow onion

1 cup finely minced carrots

3 garlic cloves, minced

1 10-ounce can tomato paste

1 750-mL bottle dry red wine

1 10.5-ounce can condensed beef consommé soup

1 pound rigatoni, cooked al dente according to package instructions

Minced fresh parsley, for garnish

Grated Parmesan cheese, for serving

1. Preheat a Dutch oven over medium heat. Next, add the ground beef and pork, pressing it into the pan to help sear the meat. Allow the meats to sear undisturbed until just beginning to smoke, 3 to 4 minutes. Using a wooden spoon, break up the meat, ensuring any pink or uncooked portions make contact with the pan to sear. Continue cooking the meats, using the spoon to break up larger chunks as necessary, until cooked through, about 10 minutes. Drain the excess fat, season with salt, pepper, and cinnamon, and stir to combine.

2. Next, stir the onions and carrots into the meat mixture and cook until tender, stirring on occasion, 4 to 6 minutes. Add the garlic and stir and cook for 60 seconds. Push the meat mixture to the perimeter of the Dutch oven, leaving an open well in the center, and add the tomato paste and toast it, stirring on occasion until it becomes pliable and loose, about 3 minutes. Deglaze by adding the wine and using a wooden spoon to scrape up any of the browned bits from the bottom of the pan. Stir in the soup, followed by a soup can full of water, and allow the mixture to return to a simmer. When the sauce reaches a low simmer, cover, reduce the heat to low, and cook for 2 to 3 hours, stirring on occasion.

3. Toss the cooked pasta into the Bolognese sauce and stir until well-incorporated. Garnish with parsley and serve with cheese, as desired.

CHICKEN AND SPINACH BAKE CASSEROLE

★ *Cheap Eats* ★ *Family-Friendly*

ADAM KLOTZ
METEOROLOGIST, FOX NEWS
&
TERRI KLOTZ
HIS MOTHER

ere's my goofy weatherman joke: Meteorologists like me know not only how to track storms, but how to cook one up too! All jokes aside, this creamy casserole is a family favorite, something my mom, Terri, dished up on "low-pressure" evenings. Honestly, my mom's been making this my whole life—and it's definitely my favorite. Frankly, if it weren't for Mama's cooking, I'd probably just be drinking a beer and eating pizza. So, I suppose I owe a lot to Mom for her quick-cook meals! Rigatoni or penne pasta is the perfect cylindrical shape for this dish to soak up the sauce and get some of that goodness into every bite. That said, if you don't have either in the pantry, you can substitute your favorite pasta, such as bowtie, macaroni, or cavatappi. In a pinch, you can skip a step by using a few cups of leftover, pulled rotisserie chicken to save some time and effort. No matter your weekday or weekend weather outlook, this dish will serve up cool breezes and sunshine in the form of a scrumptious dinner.

4 cups dried rigatoni or penne

2 boneless, skinless chicken breasts, baked and shredded

4 cups loosely packed baby spinach

1⅓ cups half-and-half

1 cup sun-dried tomatoes

1½ cups grated Parmesan cheese

Kosher salt

Fresh-cracked black pepper

1 cup shredded mozzarella cheese

1. Preheat the oven to 375°F. Lightly spray a 9 × 13-inch baking dish with cooking spray.

2. Fill a large pot with water and place over medium-high heat. When the water begins to boil, add the pasta and cook according to package instructions. Drain the pasta.

3. In a large bowl, combine the chicken, spinach, half-and-half, tomatoes, and 1 cup of the Parmesan. Toss to mix the ingredients and season to taste with salt and pepper. Add the cooked pasta and stir until evenly incorporated.

4. Next, transfer the pasta mixture to the baking dish and smooth out the top to make it even. Top the dish with the shredded mozzarella and remaining ½ cup Parmesan. Bake for 35 minutes, or until bubbly and the cheese is slightly browned on top. Cool briefly before serving.

COOKING UP A 'STORM'
FOX METEOROLOGIST TEACHES HOSTS FAMILY RECIPE

FOX NEWS channel · FOX & friends

ITALIAN MEATBALLS AND GRAVY

★ *Family-Friendly* ★ *Entertaining*

MICHAEL TAMMERO
CONSULTANT/ MARKETING EXPERT
&
BARBARA ANNE TAMMERO
HIS COUSIN

If there's anything my friends will tell you, it's that I know how to throw a great party! So, in my role here at FOX, I'm constantly looking to host fun events and also share the latest entertainment scoop and pop culture. Turns out though, I also know a thing or two in the kitchen! This dish is the perfect hearty meal for a family event; every Sunday, I never leave the apartment because I'm cooking this up to serve friends and family with a side of football. But I like to get a head start making the meatballs (a triple threat of veal, pork, and beef) the day before, allowing them to soak up extra flavor for the feast that follows. Gravy might sound like a strange term to those not of Italian or northeastern descent, but it's what makes each family recipe unique. And like most things in life, the definition of *gravy* is up for heated debate too. Most Italian American folks like me will refer to a meaty tomato sauce served on Sundays as gravy, while at other times, a meat and tomato sauce is known as ragù. Instead of debating, I'm all in for eating whatever you want to call it, especially when it's out-of-this-world good like this recipe. For me and our family, the gravy takes on a blend of traditional proteins, mixed with hot and mild Italian-style sausages and cooked as slow as your grandma walks. The results are old world, heavenly delicious.

Serves 6

MEATBALLS

½ cup pine nuts

5 slices stale white bread, crusts removed

¼ pound 80/20 ground beef

½ pound ground pork

½ pound ground veal

1 garlic clove, crushed

1½ teaspoons kosher salt

1 teaspoon fresh-cracked black pepper

1 large egg, lightly beaten

1 cup grated Parmesan cheese

One day prior to cooking, place the pine nuts and bread in a food processor and pulse to create bread crumbs. Add the bread crumb mixture and the remaining meatball ingredients to a large bowl. Using your hands, gently combine the mixture until the ingredients are evenly distributed, being careful not to overwork them. Form the mixture into meatballs, approximately 2 ounces each and 1½ inches in diameter, and place on a parchment-lined sheet pan with space between them. Cover the meatballs with plastic wrap and place in the refrigerator overnight.

BUON APPETITO!
FOX MARKETING VP MAKES CLASSIC ITALIAN DISH

FOX NEWS

FOX & friends

ITALIAN GRAVY

2 tablespoons extra virgin olive oil

1½ pounds sweet Italian sausage

1½ pounds hot Italian sausage

1 6-ounce can tomato paste

½ cup dry red wine, such as Chianti

3 28-ounce cans Italian plum tomatoes, with juice

¾ teaspoon fine sea salt

½ teaspoon fresh-cracked black pepper

3 bay leaves

1 teaspoon sugar

1½ pounds pasta (your choice), cooked according to package instructions

1. Remove the meatballs from the refrigerator and let them stand at room temperature for 30 minutes. Heat the oil in a large Dutch oven over medium heat. Add the meatballs, working in batches as necessary, and cook until golden on all sides, about 6 minutes. With a slotted spoon, transfer the lightly browned meatballs to a platter lined with paper towels.

2. Add the sausages into the same Dutch oven, cooking in batches as necessary, and brown on all sides. Using a fork, poke the sausages in several places to pierce the casing to let the fat run out. Cook the sausages, turning on occasion, for 7 to 9 minutes. Place the sausages on the platter alongside the meatballs.

3. Next, add the tomato paste into the Dutch oven and cook for 2 minutes, stirring with a wooden spoon. Deglaze by adding the red wine and stir to combine, scraping up any brown bits from the bottom of the pot. Add the canned tomatoes, crushing them by hand prior to pouring them in with their juices. Add the salt, pepper, bay leaves, and sugar and cook for 6 to 7 minutes, or until the mixture just comes to a simmer.

4. Return the browned meatballs and sausages to the sauce, pushing them down to submerge. Reduce the heat to very low and cook the sauce, uncovered, for 2 hours, stirring on occasion and being careful not to break up the meatballs. Taste the sauce, adjust the seasoning as necessary with more salt and pepper. Remove from the heat, cover, and let rest at room temperature for 1 to 3 hours. To serve, gently heat as needed and serve over hot cooked pasta.

SWEET AND SPICY CHICKEN WINGS

★ *Family-Friendly* ★ *Entertaining*

JOHN MCLEMORE
&
JOHN MCLEMORE II

GRILLING EXPERTS FOR
FOX & FRIENDS **ALL-AMERICAN SUMMER CONCERT SERIES**

Our family is known not only for crafting some of the best grills and smokers in the business, we're equally good at using said pieces of equipment to produce delicious food. These sweet and spicy wings that follow a simple three-step method for success are sure to bring some flavor to the table. First, the wings are smoked low and slow to keep them super tender. The second and final steps turn up the heat to help render off some of the additional fat to create that crispy skin before being dunked in a mixture of honey and barbecue sauce. Finger-lickin' delicious.

1. In a small bowl, mix together the pepper, onion powder, chili powder, garlic powder, and seasoned salt. Place the chicken wings in a large plastic bag, pour in the dry rub, seal the bag, and shake to coat the wings. Allow the wings to marinate at least 30 minutes at room temperature, or up to 24 hours in the refrigerator.

2. Preheat a smoker or grill to 225°F. Place the wings on the grate over indirect heat and cook for 45 minutes. Meantime, combine the honey, BBQ sauce, and apple juice together in a small sauce pan. Mix the ingredients and place on the grate over indirect heat until warmed.

2½ tablespoons fresh-cracked black pepper

1 tablespoon onion powder

1 tablespoon chili powder

1 tablespoon garlic powder

1 tablespoon seasoned salt

5 pounds chicken wings, rinsed and dried

1 cup honey

½ cup hot BBQ sauce

3 tablespoons apple juice

3. Remove the wings from the heat and place in a disposable aluminum pan. Cover the wings with the warmed sauce and toss evenly to coat.

4. Increase heat on the grill or smoker to 450°F. Place the pan of wings back on the grate and cook for 15 minutes.

5. To finish, remove the wings from the pan and cook them directly on the grate, 12 to 15 minutes, flipping constantly until the wings are seared. Remove from the grill and serve immediately.

PASTA BARNYCH

★ *Family-Friendly* ★ *Healthy*

JANICE DEAN
METEOROLOGIST, FOX NEWS

I always tell folks to be prepared, especially when it comes to stocking up for a big storm. And when the outlook isn't great, it's good to have a comfort classic on standby. Take this Dean family pasta dish, for example, as a sure cure to make an evening spent at home worth the adventure. While I'm not fully sure who to credit for this recipe, my own research has me attributing it to Yaroslav Barnych, the famous Ukrainian composer and conductor who spent much of his time in Cleveland, Ohio. He's the most famous Barnych I could find, after all! When it comes to making this pasta, don't skimp on the pine nuts. A little goes a long way, and they add a nice crunch and flavor contrast to help make this pasta dish even more special. While this meal is vegetarian friendly, there's nothing wrong with adding some grilled protein such as chicken, pulled pork, or shrimp on top, if you desire. While this can serve an army, like most pastas, it's even better the next day and makes for a fridge-ready meal that can be heated up quickly at the office or home.

Serves 10

2 pounds bowtie or penne pasta

¼ cup extra virgin olive oil

1 garlic clove, sliced

⅓ pound pine nuts

½ pound sun-dried tomatoes, packed in olive oil, chopped

1 to 1½ pounds plum tomatoes, seeded and diced

1 teaspoon kosher salt

1 teaspoon fresh-cracked black pepper

1 pound fresh mozzarella cheese, cut into ½-inch cubes

2 large bunches fresh basil, washed and cut into thin ribbons

1. Bring a large pot filled with water to a boil over medium-high heat on the stovetop. Add the pasta and cook to al dente according to package instructions. Drain the pasta and keep warm.

2. Heat the oil in a large skillet over medium heat. Add the garlic and lightly fry for 60 seconds. Add the pine nuts to the oil and garlic and sauté for 2 to 3 minutes. Next, add sundried tomatoes and half of the plum tomatoes, reduce heat to low, season with the salt and pepper, and cook for 4 to 6 minutes.

3. Add the drained pasta back into the large pot along with the remaining plum tomatoes. Pour the contents of the skillet into the pot of pasta and mix until combined. Allow the contents to cool for 2 to 3 minutes, stirring on occasion. Finish by adding the mozzarella and basil, toss to incorporate, and serve.

GLUTEN-FREE PIZZA

BRET BAIER

ANCHOR, *SPECIAL REPORT WITH BRET BAIER*

*J*ust because you are eating a bit healthier doesn't mean you need to sacrifice any flavor. That's a lesson my wife, Amy, taught me when she helped our family focus on gluten-free foods to aid in our overall health. Though Amy is 100 percent gluten free, me and my boys, Paul and Daniel, would be closer to, well, about 50 percent—but that doesn't mean we've stopped enjoying delicious meals. So yes, you can have your cake (pizza in this instance) and eat it too! This gluten-free recipe calls for a simple at-home dough, which you can make easily and customize to your liking. The great thing about pizza is that you can literally make it your own masterpiece, every time. It's the perfect catch-all meal to cook up any of the odds and ends you might have lying around in the fridge or pantry. To maintain the healthy theme, you can use a reduced-fat mozzarella cheese; I like to grate my own instead of buying the pre-grated stuff since it melts better. To get a crispy crust, I like to pre-bake the dough prior to adding the sauce and additional toppings. If you can't finish this pizza in one sitting, it reheats well in the oven or microwave for a quick lunch the following day.

1 tablespoon active dry yeast

1½ cups warm (about 110°F) water, divided

3 tablespoons sugar, divided

3 cups gluten-free flour blend

1 teaspoon kosher salt

½ teaspoon baking powder

1 tablespoon extra virgin olive oil

6 ounces gluten-free pizza sauce

4 cups shredded mozzarella cheese

Additional pizza toppings, as desired

1. Preheat the oven to 350°F. In a small bowl, combine the yeast and ¾ cup of the warm water. Allow the yeast to sit in the water for 5 minutes to activate, sprinkling in 1 tablespoon of the sugar halfway through the activation process.

2. In a medium bowl, combine the flour blend, salt, baking powder, and remaining 2 tablespoons sugar. Whisk until well blended. Make a well in the dry mixture and pour in the yeast mixture. Add the olive oil and the remaining ½ cup warm water before stirring with a wooden spoon until well combined.

3. Lightly coat a baking sheet or pizza stone with cooking spray and place the dough on top. Using your hands and working from the middle out, push to spread and flatten the dough to the edge, ideally creating a thin crust about ¼ inch in thickness.

4. Pre-bake the pizza crust for 25 to 30 minutes, or until it begins to look dry. Note that cracks might appear, which is normal.

5. Remove the pizza from the oven and spread the sauce on the crust. Top with the cheese and any other desired toppings. Bake the pizza for an additional 20 to 25 minutes, or until the edges are golden brown and the toppings are warm and bubbly. Remove the pizza from the oven, cut immediately, and serve.

INSTANT POT LAMB CHOPS

★ *Healthy* ★ *Quick Eats*

CHEF GEORGE DURAN

Lamb chops are an accessible and elegant main dish to serve to guests throughout the year. Thankfully, nowadays you can source lamb chops from most supermarkets, but specialty stores and butchers are always aiming to earn your business with some good quality cuts too. Whether broiled in the oven, prepared on the grill, or, as this recipe calls for, made in an Instant Pot, cooking delicious and impressive chops couldn't be more simple. In my experience as a chef, home cooks are often scared about how long they should cook lamb. But by leveraging the Instant Pot, you can set those fears aside and cook this dish in record time. Particularly, the Instant Pot uses both its searing and its pressure cooking ability to impart even more flavor into these delicious chops. The Instant Pot is widely available at retail outlets, as well as online, and its affordability and versatility have made it one of the more popular modern pieces of home cooking equipment. For even more deliciousness, I recommend simmering the leftover cooking liquid for a few minutes until it's reduced to a luscious sauce to serve alongside this savory main.

2 pounds lamb chops

2 tablespoons kosher salt

2 tablespoons fresh-cracked black pepper

2 tablespoons extra virgin olive oil

½ cup dry red wine

½ cup beef broth

2 sprigs rosemary

1 bay leaf

1 10-ounce box couscous, such as Near East, prepared according to package instructions

1. Arrange the lamb on a plate or baking sheet. Using a paper towel, pat the chops dry and season them evenly on both sides with the salt and pepper.

2. Turn on the sear function on your Instant Pot, add the oil, and sear both sides of the lamb chops, working in batches as needed, for 1 minute per side. Return all the seared lamb chops to the Instant Pot and add the wine, broth, rosemary, and bay leaf. Turn on the pressure cook function and cook for 3 minutes. Release the pressure, remove the chops from the Instant Pot, and serve immediately.

ESSEX, VT

LIVE | 9:56 AM ET

FOX NEWS channel

CHEF GEORGE DURAN'S TWISTS ON EASTER CLASSICS

• Happy Easter •

RICK'S STEAK TACOS

★ *Entertaining* ★ *Healthy*

RICK REICHMUTH
METEOROLOGIST, FOX NEWS

I'll be the first to admit—grilling in my NYC city apartment is easier said than done. After all, finding an outdoor grill in the city is no easy task! To solve that problem, I suggest broiling the steak and veggies in the oven to get the same effect, as the high heat from the broiler allows you to still pull off that direct heat sear. Just be sure to open a window to let the smoke out! Alternatively, a grill pan can be your best friend here too, as it can serve double-duty for searing on the stovetop, followed by a bake or broil in the oven to finish. These delicious steak tacos get some depth from my pureed marinade, and even more love from a grilled tomatillo salsa, which adds some spice and tang to help flavor each bite. I always make my own salsa, and you can take your salsa to the next level by throwing everything on the grill. If you can't find tomatillos, it's totally cool to use red tomatoes and, for an extra kick, some chipotles in adobo. You can top these meaty grilled tacos as desired, but my favorite condiments include sliced radishes, cheese, grilled onions, and lime.

Serves 6

1 medium onion, chopped

2 garlic cloves, smashed

Juice of 2 limes

1 teaspoon ground cumin

1 teaspoon kosher salt

½ teaspoon fresh-cracked black pepper

2 pounds inside skirt steak or flank steak

18 corn tortillas

FOR SERVING

Tomatillo salsa (recipe follows)

Thinly sliced radishes

Crumbled cotija cheese

Grilled green onions

1. Place the onions, garlic, lime juice, cumin, salt, and pepper into a blender and puree until smooth. Transfer the blended marinade into a large sealable plastic bag. Add the steak to the bag and toss to coat with the marinade. Seal the bags and refrigerate, turning on occasion, for at least 2 hours prior to cooking, or up to overnight.

2. Prepare a direct charcoal fire over medium-high heat, or preheat a gas grill for 10 minutes with the dials set to medium-high heat. Remove the steak from the bag, shaking off any excess marinade. Grill the meat for approximately 3 minutes per side, or as desired, and remove from grill to rest for 10 minutes. Meanwhile, place the tortillas on the grill for 30 to 45 seconds on each side, then keep the grilled tortillas warm within a folded dish towel.

3. Slice the steak very thinly on the bias to serve with the tortillas, tomatillo salsa, and additional toppings as desired.

GET THE RECIPE & VOTE AT FOXANDFRIENDS.COM

FOX & friends

TOMATILLO SALSA

8 to 10 tomatillos, husks removed and rinsed

1 onion, ends trimmed, peeled, and quartered

5 garlic cloves, skin on

2 jalapeño peppers

1 cup fresh cilantro leaves

1 teaspoon kosher salt, plus more if needed

Prepare a direct charcoal fire over medium-high heat, or preheat a gas grill for 10 minutes with the dials set to medium-high heat. Place the tomatillos, onion, garlic, and jalapeños on the grill. Grill the vegetables, turning on occasion, for 4 to 6 minutes, or until charred. Remove from the grill and allow to cool slightly. Carefully peel and remove the skin from the garlic and place the cloves in a blender with the tomatillos and onion. Cut the jalapeños in half, remove the seeds (reserve if additional spice is desired), and add to the blender. Pulse the blender for 30 seconds to break down the ingredients. Next, add the cilantro and salt and pulse until desired consistency is reached, adding more salt and jalapeño seeds to your liking.

GRILLED FLOUNDER WITH MAMA'S GRITS

★ *Entertaining*

AINSLEY EARHARDT
CO-HOST, *FOX & FRIENDS*

This is so southern, y'all. And truthfully, though I barely know how to make this flounder, I sure do know how to eat it! Growing up in Columbia, South Carolina, I have fond memories of my best friend, whose parents owned a farmers market filled with local produce. On certain special days, we would cook up a celebration on the back deck with friends, enjoying vine-ripe fresh sliced tomatoes as a side of summer. To keep the meal light and fresh, flounder fillets were cooked on the grill to serve as a main. In South Carolina, and beyond, flounder is a mild, tender fish that can be found in abundance at local markets or stores. In a pinch, you could substitute the flounder for other favorites like mahi-mahi or grouper. To make things even better, enter my creamy grits which I learned how to cook, like most of us down south, from Mama. Put a little cream in there, stir, and cook them for a loooong time. You have my word, this southern-inspired meal aims to please any night of the week.

Carley's Corner: "Sweet Ainsley," as I call her, is one of the most beautiful people, inside and out. She showcases her generosity by picking up the tab for the FOX & Friends hosts and crew regularly with Chick-fil-A biscuits to make even the most regular morning extra special.

MAMA'S GRITS

1 cup old-fashioned grits, such as Quaker

¼ teaspoon kosher salt

4 tablespoons (½ stick) unsalted butter

¼ cup heavy cream

In a small pot, bring 4 cups of water to a boil over medium-high heat. Slowly stir in the grits until well mixed, reduce the heat to low, cover, and cook, stirring occasionally, for 25 to 30 minutes. Stir in the salt, butter, and cream until the butter is melted and incorporated. Keep warm to serve.

GRILLED FLOUNDER

4 6- to 8-ounce flounder fillets

2 tablespoons extra virgin olive oil

1 lemon, cut in half

Kosher salt

Fresh-cracked black pepper

3 vine-ripened tomatoes, sliced to serve

1. Prepare a direct charcoal fire over medium-high heat, or preheat a gas grill for 10 minutes with the dials set to medium-high heat. Tear 4 large sheets of aluminum foil, and crimp the sides to create 4 boat-like vessels. Place a flounder fillet in each one of the vessels, drizzle the fillets with the olive oil and some lemon juice, and generously season with salt and pepper.

2. Place the foil vessels on the grill, cover, and cook for 6 to 8 minutes, or until the fish flakes when under light pressure. Let rest for 2 to 3 minutes.

3. Season the tomatoes with salt and pepper. Remove the fillets from the foil vessels and serve alongside the tomatoes and grits.

GRILLED RIBEYE STEAKS
WITH BLUE CHEESE BUTTER

CARLEY SHIMKUS

In my world, there are few pleasures in life that I enjoy more than a perfectly grilled steak . . . but I like to believe that perfection can be taken up a notch! Take this grilled ribeye steak, for example, which I like to cook up quickly on my charcoal-fueled grill and finish with a sultry blue cheese butter. Truthfully, some of the best steaks I've had in my life were not those from a restaurant, rather they were enjoyed in the comfort of my own home with friends and family. My secret is to source the best steaks possible, dry-aged and well-marbled for that intense beef flavor. I usually pick these up at my local butcher shop, as I find the quality to be top-notch, not to mention the fact that I like to shop local. This particular recipe calls for cooking steaks that are a bit on the thinner side, as they will cook up rather quickly, since patience isn't every cook's forte—including my own. If you are not a huge fan of blue cheese, you could substitute gorgonzola cheese for a milder flavor. Crumbled feta or goat cheese make for good, tangy substitutions—or you could skip the cheese altogether (said me, never!). I like to pair this up with some baked potatoes or dressed greens and a hearty red wine for a restaurant-quality dinner chez moi.

RIBEYE STEAKS

4 dry-aged ribeye steaks, cut less than 1 inch thick (8 to 10 ounces each)

2 tablespoons canola oil

Kosher salt

Fresh-cracked black pepper

FOR SERVING

Blue Cheese Butter (recipe follows)

Baked potatoes

1. Remove the steaks from the refrigerator at least 30 minutes prior to cooking. Drizzle with the canola oil and season both sides generously with kosher salt and fresh-cracked pepper.

2. Meanwhile, prepare a direct charcoal fire over medium-high heat, or preheat a gas grill for 10 minutes with the dials set to medium-high heat.

3. Grill the steaks, covered, over direct heat for 2 to 3 minutes per side, or until the internal temperature reaches 130°F on an instant-read thermometer for medium rare. Remove the steaks from the grill, let them rest for 5 minutes, and top each with approximately 1 tablespoon of the blue cheese butter. Serve the steaks with baked potatoes on the side.

BLUE CHEESE BUTTER

8 tablespoons (1 stick) unsalted butter, at room temperature

½ cup crumbled blue cheese

1 garlic clove, very finely minced

1 tablespoon minced fresh parsley

Combine the butter, blue cheese, garlic, and parsley in a small bowl. Using a fork, mash the ingredients together until combined. Place the butter mixture in the refrigerator to firm up.

NOTE: This butter can be prepared in advance, wrapped tightly in plastic wrap, and stored in the refrigerator for up to 1 week

GRANDMA'S CABBAGE ROLLS

★ *Family-Friendly* ★ *Comfort Food*

DR. MARC SIEGEL

MEDICAL CONTRIBUTOR, FOX NEWS

Every grandmother has her secret ingredient, and in our family, that old adage holds true for my kids too. Take, for example, my mom's not-so-obvious addition of brown sugar and cinnamon to the tomato-based sauce that makes these cabbage rolls even more sweet and savory, i.e., highly addictive. These plump rolls of cabbage stuffed with meat and rice (or as I like to say, a little bit of this, and a little bit of that) are a staple of many families like ours who trace their roots back to Eastern Europe, and each family's version is known for its distinctive flavor or twist. But for me, my wife, Ludmilla, and our three kiddos, not only is this a traditional favorite, it's a celebratory dish too. Gathering the family around to make these kinds of traditional recipes is a way to not only honor those from the past, but perhaps more importantly, to teach the traditions to the next generation. And to respect the observations of our Jewish faith, on Passover we make these delicious cabbage rolls with matzo meal, instead of the Minute rice. Just substitute 2 to 3 tablespoons of matzo meal per pound of protein to pull off the miracle. My favorite part is the leftovers, which can be reheated—or eaten cold.

1 medium cabbage, cut ½ inch from the bottom to expose the leaves

2 pounds ground beef, or ground turkey

1 cup Minute instant white rice

2 large eggs, beaten

1 tablespoon kosher salt

1½ teaspoons fresh-cracked black pepper

1½ teaspoons onion powder

1½ teaspoons garlic powder

4 28-ounce cans tomato sauce

1½ 8-ounce cans (12 ounces total) tomato paste

Juice of 1 lemon

1. Fill a large pot with water and bring to a boil over medium-high heat. Add the cabbage and boil until tender, 7 to 8 minutes. Remove the cabbage and allow it to cool to the touch. Note: Some of the cabbage leaves might fall off in the first few minutes of cooking, they can be removed when tender.

2. Meanwhile, add the beef, rice, eggs, salt, pepper, onion powder, and garlic powder to a bowl. Using your hands, gently combine the mixture, being careful not to overwork the meat.

3. In a medium pot, combine the tomato sauce, tomato paste, and lemon juice and bring to a slow simmer over medium heat.

4. Carefully peel and separate the cabbage leaves from the boiled cabbage. Stuff each leaf with 1½ to 2 tablespoons of the rice mixture, tuck in the sides, roll it up, and place seam side down into a large pot. Continue in this manner, placing the cabbage rolls side by side and stacking additional layers perpendicular, if needed. Pour the tomato sauce over the rolls and bring to a simmer over medium heat. Cover the pot, reduce the heat to low, and cook the cabbage rolls for 1½ to 2 hours, until tender.

5. To serve, remove the cabbage rolls to a plate or platter and top them with additional sauce, as desired.

Chapter 5

SNACKS & SIDES

EMANUEL FAMILY'S SPANAKOPITA

★ *Comfort Food*

MIKE EMANUEL
CHIEF WASHINGTON CORRESPONDENT, FOX NEWS

I would describe myself as a family guy, and I believe that tradition is important. That's why I keep my family's Greek heritage alive by sharing this spanakopita recipe with everyone. But I'm not the only cook in the family; my better half, my wife, Evangeline, is known not only for being a great cook, but she's also a black belt in karate. Needless to say, I complete whatever Evangeline tells me to do in the kitchen! Though I'm often on the road on assignment, Evangeline says that "staying busy and cooking a lot" is what keeps our family unit together. This staple of Greek cuisine is an American favorite too, and though the origins of the dish are difficult to trace, there's evidence of the Greeks eating a similar creation that dates back more than four hundred years. We believe our family version is authentic, and fortunately for us, we don't have to go back in time to enjoy it! Three different kinds of cheese (make sure to use a good-quality feta that's packed in brine as it will add more creaminess to the dish) and fresh spinach provide plenty of goodness. The cooking is made a bit easier by wrapping everything together in store-bought phyllo dough. I'm always the official taste-tester, and this dish has my stamp of approval. The recipe is easier to prepare than it is to pronounce, and the results are absolutely delicious.

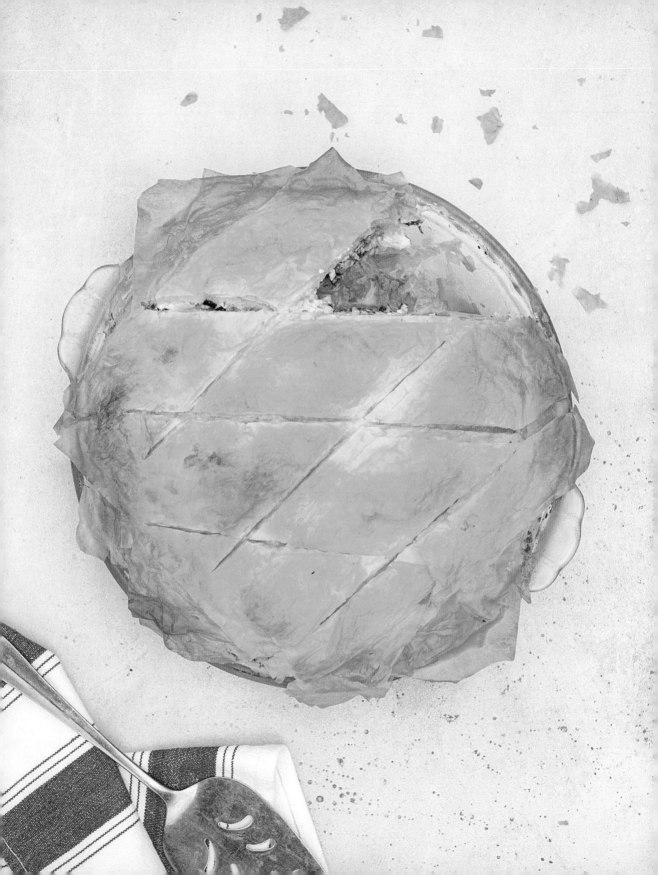

Serves 6

2 12-ounce bags fresh spinach

1 bunch fresh dill

1 bunch fresh parsley

¾ pound (3 sticks) unsalted butter

1 bunch green onions, chopped

1 pound feta cheese, crumbled

1 cup grated fontinella cheese

1 16-ounce container cottage cheese

6 large eggs, beaten

1 16-ounce package phyllo dough, thawed and covered with a dish towel to keep moist

1. Preheat the oven to 350°F. Add about ¼ inch of water to a large pot and bring the water to a boil. Add the spinach, cover the pot, and steam until the spinach is completely wilted. Drain the spinach very well and finely chop on a cutting board along with the dill and parsley. Transfer to a large bowl.

2. In a large skillet, melt 8 tablespoons (1 stick) of the butter over medium heat and cook the green onions, 5 to 7 minutes. Transfer the green onions and butter to the bowl with the spinach, dill, and parsley.

3. Using an electric hand mixer, cream together the feta, fontinella, and cottage cheeses and the eggs in a large bowl. Add the cheese mixture to the vegetable mixture and mix well.

4. To assemble, melt 8 to 16 tablespoons (1 to 2 sticks) of the butter in a small saucepan over medium heat. Use some of the butter to grease a 9 × 13-inch casserole dish. Add one layer of phyllo dough to the dish and brush the top with butter. Continue adding layers of phyllo dough and brushing them with butter until there are 7 layers in the bottom of the casserole. Spread the spinach and cheese filling on top of the phyllo base. Then, repeat with another 7 layers of phyllo dough brushed with butter.

5. Press the phyllo dough to seal the edges. Score the top layer of the filo into rectangles or triangles with a paring knife. Bake in the preheated oven for 45 to 50 minutes, or until the top is golden brown. Remove from oven and let cool for 30 minutes prior to slicing and serving.

CHALLAH BREAD

JONATHAN MORRIS

CONTRIBUTOR, FOX NEWS

I often describe the taste, texture, and experience of this challah bread with one word— "heavenly." It certainly might be, as manna, or bread, is traced back to biblical times when God sent it to the Israelites in the wilderness. Bread has often been baked and given to priests as an offering, so making this recipe can be a way of connecting with the spiritual rituals of the past. But even for a man of faith like me, time is not infinite. The trick to making this challah in less time is taking advantage of the oven in the two-step rising process. Instead of having to wait for the dough to rise at room temperature, which can take a while, a low-heated oven speeds up the initial rising process so that you can make this addictive bread in just a few hours. The honey and butter mixture provides a bit of sweet and savory with each and every bite. I suggest serving this warm, right out of the oven, alongside some wine and cheese—oh, and yes, enjoy in moderation, of course.

2½ cups warm (approximately 110°F) water

1 teaspoon sugar

3 tablespoons active dry yeast

¾ cup vegetable oil, plus more for the bowl

¾ cup honey, plus 2 tablespoons

3 large eggs

1½ tablespoons kosher salt

8 cups unbleached all-purpose flour, plus more for dusting

1 tablespoon poppy seeds

EGG WASH

2 tablespoons honey

1 large egg

1. Preheat the oven to 350°F. When it reaches that temperature, turn off the oven. Meanwhile, place the warm water in a large bowl, add the yeast and sugar and let rest until the mixture starts to bubble and grow. Next, add the oil, ¾ cup honey, 2 of the eggs, and the salt all at once and mix them together. Slowly add the flour, 1 cup at a time, mixing after each addition. When the bread dough begins to release itself from the sides of the mixing bowl, transfer the dough to a floured surface.

2. Knead the dough, adding more flour as needed to make a stand-up dough that is still slightly tacky. Lightly grease the large bowl, form the dough into a ball, and return it to the bowl. Cover the bowl with a warm, wet towel and place it in the preheated oven.

3. When the dough has doubled in size, take it out of the oven and reduce the heat to 250°F. Cut the dough into three larger balls and three smaller balls. Using your hands, roll and shape the larger balls into long strips to braid. Intertwine the long strips back and forth until the dough is braided into a loaf shape. Next, shape the smaller balls into long strips to braid. Once braided, squeeze the ends to keep them braided, and place the smaller braids on top of the larger loaf.

4. Mix together the remaining egg, 1 tablespoon of water, and the remaining 2 tablespoons honey and brush it all over the loaf. Sprinkle the poppy seeds on top.

5. Transfer the dough to a greased baking sheet and place it into the oven to rise again, 10 to 15 minutes. Raise the temperature of the oven to 375°F. Meanwhile, make the egg wash by whisking together the honey and egg in a small bowl. Bake the challah, brushing with the egg wash as it rises, for 35 to 40 minutes, or until golden brown. Serve immediately.

CUCUMBERS AND CREAM POLISH SALAD

KAT TIMPF
ANALYST, FOX NEWS

*W*hile I might be known for slinging some quick wit on topics of the day, I'm no slouch at preparing quick-fix recipes in the kitchen either. This was my mother Anne's favorite recipe, and it's now a dish that I make to honor her, and also because it's really easy to make and it goes with everything. *Mizeria* is the traditional name for this Polish combo of cucumbers and sour cream, a dish that traces its roots back several hundred years to Europe, and was made popular in Polish communities throughout America. Don't skip salting the cucumbers, as pulling out every bit of moisture will ensure that the salad comes together with integrity and crunch. If desired, you can sub in English-style cucumbers, which have fewer seeds and more consistency in shape and size. A good-quality, full-fat sour cream is preferred here, to add just the right amount of creaminess and tang to help this dish sing. This is a great cool, crunchy, and refreshing side dish to serve alongside a warm casserole or grilled main.

Serves 6

4 large cucumbers, peeled

1 teaspoon kosher salt

1 cup sour cream

1 tablespoon fresh lemon juice

1 teaspoon sugar

1 teaspoon dried dill

½ teaspoon fresh-cracked black pepper

1. Thinly slice the cucumbers, about ⅛ inch thick, and season with the salt. Allow the salted cucumbers to sit for 5 minutes. Using your hands, gently squeeze cucumbers to remove as much liquid as possible. Transfer the cucumbers to a serving bowl.

2. Add the sour cream, lemon juice, sugar, dill, and pepper, toss to combine, and serve.

NOTE: This can be prepared 1 to 2 hours in advance and kept covered in the refrigerator until ready to serve. Avoid prepping too far in advance, though, as the cucumbers will lose their crunch.

CUCUMBERS & CREAM POLISH SALAD
KAT WHIPS UP FAVORITE RECIPE FROM HER MOM
FOX & friends

GRANDMA BETT'S SUNDAY GRAVY

★ *Family-Friendly* ★ *Comfort Food*

TODD PIRO
CO-HOST, *FOX & FRIENDS FIRST*,
&
HIS FAMILY

Some folks might greet their parents with a hello, but whenever I return to the Jersey shore to visit family, my first question is, "Where's the food?" Fortunately, my parents, Pete and Marianne, get the gig, and this is often one of the dishes that awaits my arrival. Having spent most of my career in diners, I also know my way around the kitchen. Created by my grandma Bett, this slow-cooked gravy includes both hot and sweet sausages and a meatball trifecta of beef, veal, and pork in the savory sauce. As my mom will tell you, we are a family that likes to cook, eat, and enjoy ourselves. Like a true grandmother's recipe, all good things come to those who wait: the gravy is cooked low and slow (Grandpa was responsible for stirring the pot throughout the process), until it is ready to be served over cooked rigatoni, or your favorite pasta. The finale is a dollop of ricotta cheese. This Sunday-style meal has been celebrated for centuries by Italian-American families like us, and it's a ritual that's passed down generationally. Beyond the delicious food, it's the act of hospitality, of inviting friends and family over (or me crashing my mom and dad's place) to share in a good meal and fellowship, that I most admire.

Serves 4 to 6

MEAT

1 pound Italian sausage, hot, sweet or mixed

⅓ pound ground beef

⅓ pound ground veal

⅓ pound ground pork

½ cup Italian-style bread crumbs

1 large egg

2 tablespoons chopped fresh Italian parsley

¼ cup grated Parmesan cheese

½ teaspoon kosher salt

½ teaspoon fresh-cracked black pepper

1. In a large sauté pan, fry the sausages over medium heat for 3 minutes per side. Place on a paper towel–lined plate to drain.

2. Meanwhile, add the beef, veal, pork, bread crumbs, egg, parsley, Parmesan, salt, and pepper to a medium bowl. Using your hands, combine the meat mixture, being careful not to overwork it, and form it into small meatballs.

3. Add the meatballs to the sauté pan and fry for 2 minutes on each side until browned. Remove the meatballs to the plate with the sausage.

4. To prepare the sauce, heat the oil in a Dutch oven over medium-low heat. Add the onions and sauté until translucent, 5 to 7 minutes. Add the garlic and bay leaves and cook for 45 seconds. Using a wooden spoon, push the onion mixture to the sides to create a well in the center of the Dutch oven. Add the tomato paste to the center, stirring it for 1 to 2 minutes. Stir the paste into the onions and cook an additional 45 to 60 seconds.

Carley's Corner: Todd might be my co-host, but really he's like my brother. In fact, I spend more time with Todd than nearly anyone else in the world, thus we have a ton of great memories of meals shared together over the years. One time, while we were staying in Florida for the Patriot Awards, Todd would grab me breakfast from the hotel buffet. What I wasn't prepared for was the mountains of food he put on my plate—but he was just being kind by making sure I had plenty of options.

SAUCE

¼ cup extra virgin olive oil

1 medium onion, ends removed, peeled, and finely chopped

3 garlic cloves

2 bay leaves

2 6-ounce cans tomato paste

1 28-ounce can San Marzano plum tomatoes

2 tablespoons dried oregano

½ cup grated Parmesan cheese

1 teaspoon sugar

Fresh-cracked black pepper

Rigatoni, prepared according to package instructions

1 cup whole-milk ricotta cheese

5. Using your hands, squeeze the San Marzano tomatoes as you add them into the Dutch oven along with the juices from the can. Using one of the 6-ounce tomato paste cans, add 12 ounces of water to the pot and with a wooden spoon scrape up any browned bits from the bottom of the pan.

6. Next add the oregano, cheese, sugar, and pepper to taste. Stir the mixture thoroughly.

7. Add the cooked sausage and meatballs to the Dutch oven, stirring to ensure they are evenly distributed. Reduce the heat to low, partially cover the pot, and cook for 1½ to 2 hours.

8. Serve the gravy over al dente pasta with a dollop of ricotta on top.

PIROS SHARE FAMILY RECIPE

FOX&friends

FOX NEWS channel

Chapter 6

DESSERTS

GRANDMA'S APPLE CAKE

★ *Family-Friendly* ★ *Comfort Food*

CARLEY SHIMKUS

Love was in the air when my flight-attendant mom, Zulma, met my father, Ed, a passenger on one of Mom's flights. They managed to stay in touch (even before cell phones, which still blows my mind), fell in love, got married, and had my sister and me. The four of us love eating this cake all year round but especially in the autumn. The recipe has been in my family for more than fifty years. My grandmother discovered it in a local paper, but we now claim this as a Shimkus family recipe. I admit, I'm no championship baker, but this is a simple two-step recipe that comes together without a fuss. Childhood memories like picking apples and baking this cake every fall still remain strong for me, so this dish is not only delicious but also nostalgic. The crisp and tart Granny Smith apples provide just the right flavor in this cake—however, you could substitute your favorite apple variety. I also like to pretend it's healthy because there's a lot of fruit in there. If you can't wait to eat this as a dessert, I recommend having it as a quick breakfast with coffee or tea. Now that's what I call a great start to the day, folks!

Serves 6

3 large eggs

1½ cups sugar

2 cups all-purpose flour

1¼ teaspoons ground cinnamon

1 teaspoon baking soda

¼ teaspoon kosher salt

¾ cup canola oil

4 cups peeled and diced Granny Smith apples (from about 4 apples)

1 cup chopped walnuts

1. Preheat the oven to 350°F. In a medium bowl with a hand-held electric mixer at high speed, beat the eggs and sugar for 4 or 5 minutes, or until the mixture has thickened. Sift together the flour, cinnamon, baking soda, and salt. On low speed, gradually mix the flour mixture into the eggs, scraping the bowl with a spatula to ensure all the flour is incorporated. Next, add the oil and mix at medium speed until the batter is thick and smooth. Using a spatula, fold in the apples and nuts.

2. Spread the batter into 9 × 13-inch ungreased pan. Bake for 55 to 60 minutes, or until a toothpick inserted into the center comes out clean. Let rest for 15 minutes prior to serving.

GRANDMA'S APPLE CAKE
CARLEY'S "ULTIMATE COMFORT FOOD"

FIVE-MINUTE BEIGNETS

STEVE DOOCY

CO-HOST, *FOX & FRIENDS*

*T*urns out, you don't have to stand in a long line at New Orleans's famous Café du Monde to get your beignet fix. When I was covering the Super Bowl in 1997 for FOX in New Orleans, I fell in love with these sweet treats. If you are not familiar with beignets, you can use my loose definition—"French donuts." As the story goes, the origins of *beignet* can be traced to the word *bigne*, which in the Celtic language translates to "to raise." Nowadays, this deep-fried pastry, usually made from yeast dough, is most associated with France, yet it's also a staple of Cajun cuisine domestically. The genius, time-saving hack for making beignets is using store-bought biscuit dough as the base of the recipe.

This five-minute dessert is sure to become a quick-fix favorite for all your sugary cravings day or night.

Vegetable oil, for frying

½ cup sugar

1 tablespoon ground cinnamon

1 16.3-ounce can Pillsbury Grands!, such as Flaky Layers Original Biscuits

1. Add about 1½ inches of oil to a Dutch oven and place it over medium-high heat.

2. While the oil heats, mix together the sugar and cinnamon in a small bowl.

3. Remove the biscuits from the can and cut them into quarters. When the oil reaches frying temperature, approximately 350°F on a deep-fry thermometer (see Note), add the biscuit quarters in batches and fry until golden brown, 45 to 60 seconds. Remove the biscuits with a slotted spoon and place them on a wire rack to drain. Repeat until all the biscuits are fried.

4. When the biscuits have cooled to the touch, toss them in the cinnamon sugar to coat. Serve immediately.

NOTE: If you don't have a thermometer to test the oil temperature, you can dip the handle of a wooden spoon carefully into the heated oil—if bubbles form around the handle, it's go time.

VARIATION: For an even more decadent dessert, drizzle the finished beignets with chocolate or caramel sauce, and serve with whipped cream or ice cream.

GRILLED WATERMELON

★ *Family-friendly* ★ *Healthy*

CHEF MATT MOORE

Believe it or not, your grill is actually one of your most useful pieces of cooking equipment. It can be heated high to sear, covered to bake, or dialed back to low and slow to create some fall-off-the-bone goodness. But for most of us (yes, even including me), we don't utilize our grill to its full potential. That's why I wrote the book *Serial Griller,* to showcase that everything can be made better on the grill. One of my favorite go-tos when it comes to entertaining is placing fruit right on the grill. That's right, I said it—and grilled fruit should become your best friend. The high heat pulls out the natural sweetness from the fruit without the need for extra sugar. While you might have seen peaches, pineapple, or figs hit the grill, I go so far as to include watermelon in my repertoire too. The key is to use a watermelon that is just ripe—if it's gone past that stage, it will be too mushy and watery to grill. No bueno. The watermelon slices just need "a kiss" on the grill to pick up some smoke and caramelization, leaving you with a warm and cool contrast that's hard to beat. You can eat the grilled watermelon as is, or top it off with the additional components to elevate this healthy and fun dessert.

Serves 8

Vegetable oil

8 1-inch-thick seedless
watermelon wedges with rinds

½ cup vanilla whole-milk Greek
yogurt

¼ cup roasted salted pistachios,
roughly chopped

2 teaspoons finely chopped
crystallized ginger

½ teaspoon grated orange zest,
from 1 orange

Fresh-cracked black pepper

1. If using a charcoal grill, open the bottom and top
   vents completely. Light a charcoal chimney starter
   filled halfway with charcoal. When the coals are
   covered with gray ash, pour them onto the bottom
   grate of the grill. Adjust the vents as needed to
   maintain an internal temperature of 450° to
   500°F. If using a gas grill, preheat to high.

2. Oil the grates with vegetable oil. Place the
   watermelon wedges on the oiled grates and grill,
   uncovered, until grill marks appear, 1 to
   2 minutes per side.

3. Place a grilled watermelon wedge on each serving
   plate. Divide the yogurt evenly among the
   wedges, garnish with the pistachios, ginger, and
   orange zest, and finish with fresh-cracked pepper
   to taste.

ANNETTE'S SOUR CREAM COFFEE CAKE

ANNETTE BRIGANTI
FRIEND OF *FOX & FRIENDS*

This is always a family favorite." While this cake goes great with a hot cup of coffee, the truth is it can be enjoyed with any beverage, any time of the day. The addition of sour cream provides some rich, tangy flavor to the batter while ensuring the cake turns out moist and perfect every time. The marbling technique typically references swirling together two different colors of batter, but for this cake, marbling means actually incorporating the nut filling into the layers to make sure you get some of the savory and sweet goodness in every bite. Made up of kitchen staples and other accessible ingredients, this is a simple recipe that always delivers.

CAKE

½ pound (2 sticks) unsalted butter, at room temperature, plus more if needed

2 cups granulated sugar

4 large eggs

1 tablespoon baking powder

1 tablespoon baking soda

4 cups all-purpose flour

2 cups sour cream

NUT FILLING

½ cup sugar

1 cup chopped walnuts

1 heaping tablespoon ground cinnamon

1. Preheat the oven to 350°F. Grease a 10-inch Bundt pan with butter or cooking spray.

2. Make the cake: Using an electric hand mixer, mix the butter, sugar, and eggs in a medium bowl until smooth. In a separate bowl, sift together the baking powder, baking soda, and flour. Add the flour mixture and sour cream to the butter mixture in alternating ½-cup increments until no more flour or sour cream remains.

3. Make the nut filling and assemble the cake: Mix together the sugar, walnuts, and cinnamon. Next, add half of the batter mixture to the pan, smoothing the top with a spatula, and evenly sprinkle with half of the nut filling. Pour the remaining batter on top, followed by a sprinkle of the remaining filling. With a butter knife, swirl the batter with the nut filling, using a zigzag motion to create a marbled effect.

4. Bake in the preheated oven for 1 hour, or until a toothpick inserted into the center of the cake comes out clean. Let rest for 15 minutes or allow the cake to come to room temperature before serving.

Chapter 7

HOLIDAYS

CHRISTMAS BREAKFAST CASSEROLE

★ *Family-Friendly* ★ *Comfort Food*

RACHEL CAMPOS-DUFFY

CO-HOST,
FOX & FRIENDS WEEKEND

While I know my way around the kitchen, on Christmas and other holidays I just want to spend as much time as possible with the kids and family. So, I've created this make-ahead favorite that can be heated the morning of to ensure everyone enjoys a comforting meal without too much time in the kitchen. If you are like-minded, I suggest making the casserole the night before, leaving it in the fridge until it's time to heat up, and serving it alongside a fruit salad—which can also be prepared ahead of time. The ingredients listed are simply a guide; you can throw in other odds and ends as you wish to build on the recipe. Candidly, you can do whatever you want with this casserole. You don't want to be fussing around here—you just want to enjoy!

While this dish is celebrated on holiday occasions in our household, you can serve it any time of the year when a bit of pre-prep might make your following morning more enjoyable.

Carley's Corner: **I will always be grateful for all of the "mom" advice Rachel has shared with me. It has made a lasting impression, especially as I begin my own journey into motherhood. My favorite mantra she told me is, "As a mom, it's not your job to get your child into Harvard, it's your job to get them into heaven." I love that. Oh, and Rachel's Parmesan-sprinkled bread-and-butter pickles, baked in the oven, was another hot tip. I craved them hard, especially during my pregnancy. Simply delish!**

Serves 8

6 slices white sandwich bread

1 pound breakfast sausage

4 scallions, white and pale green parts and dark green parts separated and thinly sliced

1 10-ounce package frozen spinach, thawed and squeezed completely dry

2 cups shredded cheddar cheese

8 large eggs

1½ cups whole milk

½ cup whole-milk Greek yogurt

1 teaspoon mustard powder

½ teaspoon kosher salt

½ teaspoon fresh-cracked black pepper

¼ teaspoon ground nutmeg

1. Preheat the oven to 425°F. Place the bread on a rimmed baking sheet and toast in the oven until dry, 8 to 10 minutes. Remove from the oven and turn off heat.

2. Meanwhile, heat a large skillet over medium-high heat. Add the sausage and cook, breaking it into pieces with a spatula, until browned, about 5 minutes. Add the white and pale green scallion parts and cook until softened, about 3 minutes. Stir in the spinach and cook until warmed through, about 2 minutes.

3. Spray a 3-quart baking dish with cooking spray and arrange the toasted bread slices in the bottom of the dish. Using a slotted spoon, scatter the sausage-and-spinach mixture over the bread layer. Sprinkle the shredded cheese over the top.

4. In a large bowl, whisk together the eggs, milk, yogurt, mustard powder, salt, pepper, and nutmeg. Gently pour the egg mixture over the casserole, cover with the lid or plastic wrap, and place in the refrigerator for at least 4 hours or up to overnight.

5. To cook, uncover the dish and transfer to a cold oven. Heat the oven to 375°F and bake the casserole until the eggs are puffed and the cheese is browned, about 40 minutes.

6. Let the casserole cool for 10 minutes. Top with the dark green scallion parts prior to serving.

HALLOWEEN SLOPPY JOES

★ *Cheap Eats* ★ *Family-Friendly* ★ *Comfort Food*

CARLEY SHIMKUS

An evening of trick-or-treating can work up quite an appetite, and in my neighborhood, it's no secret that my house is always the spot where friends drop by for an impromptu dinner to count candy and award the best costume. Okay, maybe enjoy a cocktail too. Instead of a complicated meal, I like to cook up these sloppy joes, since they are affordable, come together quickly, and can be kept warm in a slow cooker for folks to help themselves throughout the evening. While there are many variations to this dish, the sweet and savory combo of beef and sauce is a comfort classic—but you could, of course, substitute ground turkey. And since I'm usually the one footing the bill for my friends (love y'all!), serving this dish as a main is also a great way to stretch a buck, as the ingredients themselves are inexpensive and dishing them out in this saucy mixture helps them go a long way. You can round out the meal with assorted chips and pickles to serve on the side.

Serves 8

2 pounds lean ground beef

½ yellow onion, diced

1 green bell pepper, seeds removed and diced

½ teaspoon kosher salt

½ teaspoon fresh-cracked black pepper

3 garlic cloves, minced

1 cup ketchup

2 tablespoons yellow mustard

2 tablespoons light brown sugar

2½ tablespoons chili powder

1 tablespoon Worcestershire sauce

2 tablespoons tomato paste

1 dash Tabasco sauce

Hamburger buns, warmed

1. In a large Dutch oven over medium heat, brown the ground beef, using a wooden spoon to break it up, 4 to 6 minutes. Add the onion and bell pepper and season with salt and black pepper. Cook the beef and vegetables, stirring on occasion, until the vegetables are just tender, about 6 minutes. Add the garlic, stir, and cook for 60 seconds.

2. Next, add the ketchup, mustard, brown sugar, chili powder, Worcestershire, tomato paste, and Tabasco. Stir until incorporated and cook for 2 minutes. Add 1 cup of water to deglaze the pan, using a wooden spoon to scrape up any browned bits from the bottom. Reduce the heat to low, cover the pot, and simmer for 20 minutes to allow the flavors to meld.

3. Remove the cover, turn off the heat, and allow the mixture to cool and thicken for 5 minutes (see Note). Serve by spooning the mixture into the hamburger buns.

NOTE: The cooked meat mixture can be transferred to a slow cooker and kept warm on the low setting.

THANKSGIVING STUFFING AND PINK JELL-O

★ *Comfort Food* ★ *Cheap-Eats*

PETE HEGSETH
CO-HOST,
FOX & FRIENDS WEEKEND

Everybody loves Thanksgiving. And throughout most of my life, the Hegseth clan always returned to Wanamingo, Minnesota, to visit my grandmother on every Thanksgiving holiday. As is the tradition in most families, our family, including my younger brother Phil, gathered to enjoy food, family, football, and fun each holiday. When Grandma passed (a wonderful woman who lived a rich life), our family continued to honor her by cooking up these delicious favorites. One of them is Pink Jell-O, which looks absurd, but I assure you is delicious. It's both a side and dessert, something Phil enjoys to this day at the kids table. Love you, bro. I suggest a heaping portion of Pink Jell-O on your plate so that you can dip all of your favorites into it, including my grandmother's stuffing. For me, it's these unique family creations—albeit some of them a bit strange to outsiders—that makes holidays and traditions so important. Give this Pink Jell-O a try at your next family gathering—and like us, you might just have a new favorite dish to add some fun to your treasured gatherings.

THANKSGIVING STUFFING

Serves 8

½ cup margarine

5 large celery stalks, finely chopped

1 large onion, ends removed and peeled and finely chopped

1 teaspoon dried thyme

¾ teaspoon kosher salt

½ teaspoon fresh-cracked black pepper

½ teaspoon dried sage

1 14.5-ounce can chicken broth

2 loaves firm white bread, sliced into cubes

½ cup loosely packed fresh parsley leaves, chopped

1. Preheat the oven to 325°F. In a 12-inch skillet, melt the margarine over medium heat. Add the celery and onions and sauté for 12 to 15 minutes, or until tender, stirring occasionally.

2. Stir in the thyme, salt, pepper, sage, chicken broth, and ½ cup of water. Remove the skillet from the heat.

3. Place the bread cubes in a very large bowl. Add the celery mixture and parsley, toss to incorporate. Spoon the stuffing into a 9 × 13-inch glass baking dish. Cover with foil and bake for 45 minutes. Remove from the oven, uncover, and cool slightly. Serve.

PINK JELL-O

Serves 8

1 box strawberry Jell-O

1½ cups Cool Whip

Prepare the Jell-O according to box instructions. When firm, fold in the Cool Whip. Beat the mixture until blended and refrigerate until firm. Serve.

TURKEY AND SAUSAGE GUMBO

★ *Family-Friendly* ★ *Comfort Food*

CARLEY SHIMKUS

At my house, I like to skip the turkey sandwiches and make gumbo instead. Nothing against turkey sandwiches, but this thick, okra-laden dish is the perfect comforting way to bring new life to those turkey leftovers. And honestly, this day-after dish is one that my family requests the most, especially while watching a weekend of college and NFL football. If you've never made gumbo before, don't worry—I've got your back. The key to any gumbo is a good roux—an equal mixture of flour and fat cooked slowly until the color of a dull penny. Be careful though, if the roux begins to smoke and burn, you have to start the whole process over. Roux makes up the base of much of Cajun cuisine, as it serves double duty as both a punch of flavor and a thickening agent. After that, another classic combination known as the trinity (onion, bell pepper, and celery) is added to the roux, which creates a heavenly smell in the kitchen, not to mention adds even more flavor to the dish. The reserved dark meat from the turkey is usually the most sought-after in this gumbo, as it remains rich and moist in the dish—however, any leftover turkey can be tossed in alongside some spicy andouille sausage for an added kick. Serve this up with a cold beer—especially if the in-laws are still staying at your house through the weekend.

Serves 6

½ cup all-purpose flour

½ cup vegetable oil

1 large onion, ends removed and peeled and chopped

5 large celery stalks, chopped

1 green bell pepper, seeded and cored, chopped

1 bay leaf

1 teaspoon Creole seasoning

5 garlic cloves, minced

1 14.5-ounce can diced tomatoes

1 cup amber beer, such as Abita

32 ounces chicken stock

2 cups chopped okra

1½ pounds reserved turkey, chopped

1 pound andouille sausage, sliced thin

2 cups green onions, sliced and divided

Hot cooked rice, to serve

1. In a Dutch oven over medium-low heat, combine the flour and oil and whisk until incorporated. Cook the roux, stirring often, until golden brown, removing from the heat after about 15 minutes.

2. Add the onion, celery, and bell pepper and stir into the roux. Increase the heat to medium, add the bay leaf, and season with Creole seasoning. Cook until the vegetables are softened, about 7 minutes. Add garlic and cook for 1 minute.

3. Add the tomatoes and beer to deglaze the Dutch oven, using a wooden spoon to scrape up any browned bits from the bottom of the pan. Add chicken stock and allow the mixture to come to a slow boil.

4. Add the okra, return to a slow boil, cover, and reduce the heat to medium-low and simmer until the okra is tender, about 20 minutes. Add the turkey, sausage, and 1 cup of the green onions and cook, covered, on low heat for 30 minutes.

5. Prior to serving, use a spoon to skim any foam or grease from the top of the pot and discard. Serve the gumbo with the remaining green onions as garnish topped with hot cooked rice.

Chapter 8

DRINKS

ALOHA SMOOTHIES

DANIEL HOFFMAN
CONTRIBUTOR, FOX NEWS

Serves 1

1 cup cubed fresh pineapple

1 cup trimmed and quartered fresh strawberries

1 banana, peeled and sliced

1 cup low-fat vanilla Greek yogurt

1½ cups ice

⅓ cup pineapple juice

1 tablespoon vanilla protein powder (optional)

This is a little Hawaiian-inspired smoothie that can be enjoyed any time of the day. My late wife, Kim Hoffman's sister was "unfortunately" stationed in Oahu, which allowed us to take advantage of paradise while also discovering this drink during our visits. And because we sometimes have a couple of younger picky eaters in the family, this recipe allowed Kim and me to fill up the boys and sneak in a bit of fruit too. I like to imagine myself sitting on Waikiki Beach every time I enjoy this tropical treat. But if sitting on the beach and enjoying fruity drinks is not your thing, you can also turn this into a satisfying post-workout drink by adding the optional protein powder. Hmm, spiking it with rum sounds like a good idea too! In a pinch (or to change things up a bit), orange juice can be subbed for the pineapple juice. Feel free to add your favorite array of fruit to make this your own. You can also substitute frozen fruits, so you can always have the makings of this smoothie ready to rock and roll.

Place all the ingredients into a blender and puree until smooth. Transfer to your choice of drinking glass and enjoy.

KENTUCKY MULE

MARIE HARF
CONTRIBUTOR, FOX NEWS RADIO

Serves 1

1 lime wedge

3 sprigs fresh mint

2 ounces bourbon

4 ounces chilled ginger beer

Crushed ice

In honor of the great state of Kentucky, bourbon is substituted for the traditional vodka in this take on a Moscow mule. Truth be told, this drink has little to do with Moscow (or Kentucky), and more to do with New York. In the early 1940s, a struggling ginger beer entrepreneur was trying to find a way to convince a larger audience to consume the beverage. At the Chatham hotel in Manhattan, eventually served with hors d'oeuvres, the ginger beer was combined with vodka, garnished with wedges of lemon, and the Moscow mule as we know it was born. Frankly, this drink goes well with anything (including food), but I will once again endorse a "healthy pour" of the Kentucky bourbon. Make it authentic, y'all. Enjoy this creative spin on a cocktail classic, perhaps at your next kickoff party to celebrate the famous Kentucky Derby!

In a Moscow mule mug, muddle the lime wedge and leaves from two of the mint sprigs. Add the bourbon, ginger beer, and crushed ice, stirring to incorporate. Garnish with the remaining fresh mint sprig and serve.

**TEQUILA SPARKLING
JALAPEÑO LEMONADE**

SEE PAGE 236

NEW YEAR'S EVE COCKTAILS

★ *Entertaining*

CARLEY SHIMKUS

Each serves 1

Nothing gets you ready for a new year than a blend of a few spirits mixed into your favorite cocktails. When I'm hosting a New Year's Eve party, I like to give my guests options, and the following cocktails will ensure there's something for everybody to enjoy. From classics like a negroni spiked with coffee (caffeine and booze, that's one way to get the party started!), to a spicy sparkling lemonade, to a warm toddy, and finally—the hair of the dog— a breakfast cocktail, these recipes will inspire you to make the most of your last evening of the year, including a boozy start to the year ahead. In addition to these great cocktails, I have also laid out recipes for a honey syrup, simple syrup, and fresh cucumber juice, which can be used to your liking in an array of other cocktails. These supporting recipes typically keep for a week or so, meaning you can still enjoy your labor in a midweek pick-me-up. I like to say enjoy everything in moderation, so enjoy these responsibly in the new year and beyond.

CAMPARI NYE NEGRONI

1 ounce Campari

1 ounce gin, such as London Dry

1 ounce cold-brew coffee

½ ounce simple syrup
(recipe follows)

Combine all of the ingredients in a cocktail shaker with ice and shake vigorously. Strain the liquid into a martini coupe glass and serve.

NYE TODDY

2 ounces Scotch whisky, such as Macallan Rare Cask

2 ounces hot water

¼ ounce honey syrup (recipe follows)

1 dash Angostura bitters

GARNISHES

Lemon wedge

3 allspice berries

1 star anise

1 cinnamon stick

Clove-studded orange peel

In a stemless burgundy red wine glass, combine all ingredients, stirring until incorporated. Add garnishes, as desired, and serve.

TEQUILA SPARKLING JALAPEÑO LEMONADE

3 slices fresh jalapeño chile

1½ ounces silver tequila, such as Roca Patrón

1 ounce coconut water

½ ounce fresh lemon juice

½ ounce simple syrup (recipe follows)

2 ounces club soda

Lemon wedge, for garnish

In a cocktail shaker, muddle the jalapeño. Next, add the tequila, coconut water, lemon juice, and simple syrup with ice and shake vigorously. Strain the liquid into a glass over fresh ice. Top with club soda, stir, and serve, garnished with the lemon wedge.

BREAKFAST COCKTAIL

1½ ounces vodka, such as Elit

1 ounce fresh cucumber juice (recipe follows)

½ ounce simple syrup (recipe follows)

¼ ounce fresh lemon juice

3 ounces Champagne

Cucumber slices

Fresh basil leaves

Combine the vodka, cucumber juice, simple syrup, and lemon juice in a cocktail shaker with ice and shake vigorously. Strain the liquid into a glass over fresh ice. Add the Champagne and stir. Garnish with sliced cucumber and fresh basil leaves and serve.

HONEY SYRUP

4 ounces water

4 ounces honey

Bring the water to a boil over medium-high heat. Add the honey and stir until dissolved. Cool to room temperature. Honey syrup can be covered and refrigerated for up to 2 weeks.

SIMPLE SYRUP

4 ounces water

4 ounces granulated sugar

Bring the water to a boil over medium-high heat. Add the sugar and stir until dissolved. Cool to room temperature. Simple syrup can be covered and refrigerated for up to 4 weeks.

CUCUMBER JUICE

1 large cucumber

½ cup water

Wash and cut the cucumber into pieces, leaving the skin on, into pieces and place in a blender with enough water to cover the blades. Blend until smooth. Strain the liquid through a fine mesh strainer, discarding the solids. Cucumber juice can be covered and refrigerated for up to 3 days.

ACKNOWLEDGMENTS

I have been blessed with a wonderful family as well as friends and coworkers who have become family. To my husband Pete, thank you so much for being my biggest cheerleader, for making me laugh like no one else can, for eating all my meals (even the questionable ones) and going back for seconds. I can never tell if you truly like my cooking that much or are just trying to boost my confidence, but that is simply the kind of husband you are. I have loved watching you become a father to Brock, and I can't wait to continue life's journey hand in hand with you.

Mom and Dad, thank you for all of the home-cooked meals we've shared together. Whether it's Dad cooking those giant shrimp on the barbeque or Mom letting me stay home from school one day each year to bake Christmas cookies, you have both played starring roles in some of the greatest memories of my life. Thank you for being the best parents a girl could ask for.

To the incredible team at FOX News and HarperCollins who made this cookbook possible. Lauren Petterson, there is no one in the world as kind and talented as you. Thank you so much for believing in me and for all the guidance and advice along the way. Lisa Sharkey, you are incredible and your way with words is truly unmatched. Thank you so much for all of your support and for showering baby Brock with so many books. He is going to be the best little reader because of you! A very special thank you to Michael Tammero, you are one of a kind wonderful. Thank you for showing me kindness throughout my career. Kim Capasso, you have the patience of a saint. Thank you for holding my hand throughout this journey. Matt Moore, there is no greater chef than you! I have loved working with you.

To my *FOX & Friends* family, I am so blessed to have you all in my life. Todd, I laugh every morning because of you. You are simply the best. Steve, Ainsley,

Brian, Rachel, Pete, Will, and Janice, thank you for being the greatest teachers in the world. I learn every single day as I watch you shine on and off camera. Our fearless leader Gavin Hadden, your guidance and support mean more to me than you know. There would be no *FOX & Friends* without you! Sarah Popple, thank you for everything. You are going to take over the world one day. I am so lucky to know you, work with you, and call you a friend.

An extra special thanks to you, dear reader, who let all of us on FOX News be a part of your home. I hope this cookbook makes your life more delicious!

INDEX

E

F

ABOUT THE AUTHOR

CARLEY SHIMKUS is the host of *FOX & Friends First* and newsreader on *FOX & Friends*. She is a frequent guest on many shows in the FOX News lineup including *America's Newsroom*, *Outnumbered*, *Gutfeld!*, and *Hannity*. She has been working at FOX News since 2009 after graduating from Quinnipiac University with a degree in broadcast journalism. Carley lives in New York with her husband, Peter, and son, Brock.

Flags and various gingham patterns:
Ratselmeister/Shutterstock, Inc.; Anya D/Shutterstock, Inc.;
Ramona Kaulitzki/Shutterstock, Inc.

HarperCollins books may be purchased for educational, business, or sales
promotional use. For information, please email the Special Markets Department
at SPsales@harpercollins.com.

FOX News Books imprint and logo are trademarks of FOX News Network LLC.

FIRST EDITION

Book design by Shubhani Sarkar, sarkardesignstudio.com

Food photography by Andrea Behrends

Library of Congress Cataloging-in-Publication Data has been applied for.

ISBN 978-0-06-322599-2

23 24 25 26 27 TC 10 9 8 7 6 5 4 3 2 1